20TH CENTURY MILITARY
UNIFORMS

20TH CENTURY MILITARY
UNIFORMS

CHRIS MCNAB

BARNES & NOBLE BOOKS
NEW YORK

This edition published by Barnes & Noble, Inc.,
by arrangement with Amber Books Ltd
2002 Barnes & Noble Books

M 10 9 8 7 6 5 4 3 2

ISBN: 0-7607-3094-6

Reprinted in 2005

Editorial and design by
Amber Books Ltd
Bradley's Close
74–77 White Lion Street
London N1 9PF
www.amberbooks.co.uk

Project Editor: Charles Catton
Editor: Vanessa Unwin
Design: Mike Rose

Printed in Singapore

PICTURE CREDITS
TRH Pictures

ARTWORK CREDITS
De Agostini UK Ltd and Aerospace Publishing

CONTENTS

Introduction

The historical study of military uniforms has a broader significance than is commonly appreciated. A military uniform, after all, signals the practical, regimental, even ideological priorities of the soldier on the battlefield. Thus, as we cast our eye over the history of military clothing, we see not only the display of regimental pride or ethos, but also a barometer for the changes in warfare itself. Shifts in battlefield technology and tactics have demanded new modes of dress and equipment and new ways of understanding the nature of armed conflict.

Nowhere is this change better illustrated than in the transformations in uniform design within the twentieth century. During World War I, particularly in 1914 and 1915, an officer belonging to the Austrian Hussars would often be seen in battle in a striking blue Attila jacket with gold braiding, scarlet pantaloons, a ceremonial cutlass slung on his hip, and sometimes the elaborate shako helmet complete with its high crest and ornamental feathers. This spectacle would have been quite usual on the battlefields of the eighteenth and nineteenth centuries. Now move forward in time 75 years and witness a modern 'cavalryman' of a US armoured unit in the deserts of Kuwait during the Gulf War. The change could not be more dramatic: a khaki camouflage

Above: A British Tommy prepares some warm food on the Western Front during World War I. He is wearing a scarf as well as his standard issue British uniform.

clothing system with curious black and white spots, known as a 'Chocolate Chip' pattern. This uniform, shared by almost all US troops in the theatre, contained advanced fire-resistant materials; fabrics which can let out perspiration but keep out rainwater droplets; a kevlar combat helmet, part of the advanced PASGT (Personal Armor System, Ground Troops) body armour; equipment carried in a tactical load-carrying vest; minimal insignia.

The contrast is striking not just visually, but also for the massive shift in priorities. The Hussar's uniform celebrates his regiment; he wants to be seen, respected, even feared by the enemy, and expects to make his impact as an individual warrior on the battlefield: he exudes the martial spirit. The uniform of the US soldier in the Gulf War, however, speaks of the functional and the anonymous. The camouflage uniform and body armour acknowledge that he is vulnerable to modern weapons: being conspicuous means being killed. The quantity of high-tech equipment and weaponry he carries testifies to the fact that, in many cases, technology exercises a greater influence over the battlefield than pure personal valour. The fighting spirit is still there, but it is tempered by the realism of the battlefield.

The final demise of the ceremonial element in combat uniforms (not, of course, full dress uniforms) is the thread running through the history of twentieth-century uniforms. Yet uniforms did not become any less important as the century went on. As we shall see, in terms of blunt survivability, the uniform became much more integral to the soldier's role.

1914–1945: FROM KHAKI TO CAMOUFLAGE

Of all the conflicts in the twentieth century, World War I had the most seminal effect on military clothing designers. The onset of war in 1914 saw the Allied and Axis armies displaying the full spectrum of uniform types. For the common infantryman, the period 1850 to 1914 was one in which a plain style of uniform was introduced into most major armies. These uniforms were usually in khaki, field-grey or olive-drab, and featured single-breasted jackets worn with trousers or pantaloons (the latter requiring puttees or gaiters). Headgear was usually one of three types: peaked cap, field cap or steel helmet. Thus, French infantry entered the war in the blue-grey service dress adopted in 1870, the British stepped into khaki in the late 1800s in India (this extending outwards into the rest of the army in 1902), Bulgaria donned a Russian-style grey-green uniform in 1908, and Russia itself introduced khaki in 1913.

Though there were distinct and recognizable differences between uniforms, standardization was taking place. The reasons for this lie in the main in what the historian John Keegan has called the 'militarization of Europe' in the nineteenth century. A massive expansion in population (Germany doubled its population between 1870 and 1900), improvements in health and nutrition, greater wealth amongst European nations thanks to greater tax revenues (which translated into military expenditure), advanced census-taking which aided effective conscription, the ideological appeal of common military service given to the nation state: all of these factors fed into a massive increase in the number of soldiers in service. When World War I began in 1914, some 20 million European men entered into the ranks of the armed forces.

Logistics alone demanded standardization of uniforms. Ornate uniforms simply could not be made with the requisite speed,

Above: Men of the German Africa Corps with an Italian colonial during World War II.

quantity or economy to equip the new mass armies. The hordes of soldiers who entered World War I were mainly dressed in plain tunics and trousers, although many older regiments distinguished themselves with the brighter and more defiant uniforms of yesteryear. The cavalry were particularly vivid. Germany, for example, had various cavalry units, each wearing bright regimental tunics and trousers and tall head-dress, such as the shako. However, bright red or blue tunics provided an irresistible draw to the sights of enemy infantry. The first recognition that the ceremonial dress was inappropriate came with the introduction of a khaki cover for the head-dress, but by the end of 1915 most cavalry regiments wore regular army uniforms (at the same time as they were dismounting their horses). Frontline officers of all arms-of-service, with the exception perhaps of the navy, were also toning down their tendency to dress boldly, as enemy snipers found distinguishing clothing helpful in working out priority targets.

The lesson of World War I for military outfitters was that in an age of mechanized warfare and accurate rifled weapons, being highly visible was a strong disadvantage. Thus by 1918, plain uniforms were the norm across almost all armies and regiments.

Note, however, that camouflage did not make a significant appearance in the ranks of infantry during World War I. Modern disruptive-pattern camouflages were first designed for covering artillery, tanks, aircraft and ships from aerial-, ground- or ship-based reconnaissance. The only use applied to uniforms was in 1916 when some German *Sturmtruppen* units put a green, brown and grey fragmented pattern on the new *Stahlhelm* steel helmet.

It would be the interwar period in which camouflage for soldiers truly took hold. Several influential books on camouflage were published, such as Abbott H. Thayer's *Concealing Colouration in the Animal Kingdom, an Exposition of the Laws of Disguise Through Colour and Pattern* (1909) and Lieutenant-Colonel Le Marchand and E. Denis' *La Guerre Documentée* (c. 1920), which started to attract the attention of uniform designers and military thinkers. In 1929 the Italian Army issued a camouflaged tent-cloth called the *tela mimetizzata* (camouflaged cloth), and in 1930 the German forces produced a triangular poncho/tent sheet called a *Zeltbahn*. The pattern which derived from this was called Zeltbahn 31 and consisted of green and brown angular shapes against a tan background, with short, rainlike green streaks breaking up the lines in a dense pattern. This became known as Splitter (splinter) pattern, which was used on World War II uniforms issued for some Wehrmacht soldiers on the Eastern Front, to paratroopers during the invasion of Crete in 1941, and also in a softer *Sumpfmuster* (swamp pattern) variant to various infantry units in 1943.

Above: US infantrymen in Vietnam attempt to contact their base.

Nazi Germany was to stay at the forefront of camouflage uniform design, far ahead of any other army. The Waffen-SS in particular was a pioneer, especially through the input of *SS-Sturmbannführer* Wim Brandt and his assistant Professor Otto Schick. From 1937 they produced a range of foliage-pattern camouflages (mainly the *Platanenmuster* (plane tree), *Palmenmuster* (palm tree) and *Eichenlaubmuster* (oak leaf)) which closely imitated nature, camouflages which were later estimated to reduce unit casualties by 15 per cent in combat. As many as 33,000 camouflage smocks had been delivered to the Waffen-SS by September 1940 alone.

Yet World War II was still not to be the war of camouflage. As in World War I, olive-drab, khaki and field-grey predominated in the infantry, while blues, blacks, greys and whites were chief amongst the air forces and navies of the warring nations. In the European and Soviet theatres soldiers travelled through multiple terrains, from beach to woodland to mountain to city, and no uniform could be found that would provide camouflage in all these environments. However, the value of camouflage was realized for particular units in limited environments. Thus the main other user of camouflage was the US for its Pacific campaigns, particularly for the use of Raider, Airborne, sniper and Marine soldiers on the tropical Pacific islands, where jungle foliage was common. The British Army in the Far East also made a gesture towards camouflage by introducing a green version of the khaki battledress, and Russian ski-troops wore all-white ski-suits.

What World War II did do for the progression of uniform design was to advance the specialization of uniforms. The advent of total war meant that new forms of soldiering were introduced, with the accompanying requirement for new types of uniform. High-altitude strategic bombing meant that aircrew needed insulated flying suits, some Allied versions coming with electrical heating. Airborne forces required parachute uniforms with special windproof jump-smocks and cutaway helmets which would not snag on parachute lines. Tank crews needed their own specific overalls and jackets. As the number and type of regiments expanded with new types of regimental purpose, so to did the range of military insignia and colour schemes.

Load-carrying equipment also underwent changes. During World War I leather webbing systems were dominated, usually consisting of a belt and shoulder-straps on which all utility and ammunition items would be hung. Ammunition was almost invariably rifle ammunition, so bandoliers tended to be the most common way of storing rounds, individual pouches usually holding about five rounds each. New personal weapons in World War II required new systems of carriage. Submachine guns became common issue, thus longer pouches were required to hold magazines of 25–35 rounds capacity and more. Soldiers often had to traverse greater distances with mobile fronts (an effect of the domination of armour), and so packs were enlarged for most infantry.

World War II came to an end with the realization that the uniform of a soldier must contribute to his actual combat performance, rather than just provide a means of identification and basic environmental protection. This lesson was taken to heart in the post-war period with increasing sophistication.

POST-WAR DEVELOPMENTS

Revolution in uniforms naturally did not take place straight away. During the second half of the twentieth century, standardization actually continued on a global scale. There are two primary causes. First, the end of the war released massive amounts of war surplus, especially in former European colonies. Thus we see British Army khaki worn in places as disparate as Greece, India, Pakistan, Iraq, Africa and Malaya well into the 1970s, with the British 1938-pattern webbing still in use in many places today. Secondly, the onset of the Cold War started a global chess game in which the United States, the USSR and China sponsored various proxy wars with military supplies. For example, South Korean soldiers in the 1950s could be seen in US M1943 combat uniform, while their North Korean opponents would be in Chinese khaki battledress.

These two forces of standardization exercised their influence worldwide, not only making soldiers within nations look the same or similar, but also making soldiers of different nations resemble one another. The growth of guerrilla warfare in the post-war world has also meant that we see items from various Cold War military sources in unlikely combination, revolutionary fighters or terrorists utilizing whatever military stock is at hand.

What becomes apparent in the post-war period is that wealth has become the defining factor in the sophistication of uniforms. Today many developing countries in the Middle East and Africa have uniforms similar to those seen during World War II, but the same cannot be said for the developed world. The United States soon took the lead with its M1943 uniform. This adopted a layered approach to uniforms, based on the principle that many thin layers give better temperature control than few thick ones. The success of the M1943 model caught on, the UK and other European countries either buying the uniform direct or developing versions of their own. From this point on – particularly from the 1960s – the world's developed nations pushed ahead with uniform design at a rapid rate. By the 1970s, camouflage had become standard in many nations: the UK with its Disruptive Pattern Material (DPM); the US its special forces 'Tigerstripe' in Vietnam, later bringing in the M81 Woodland pattern for most soldiers in the US Army; the USSR having its 'jigsaw' and leaf patterns. By 1990, over 350 camouflages were in use throughout the world (a large percentage in the modern Russia and the former Soviet republics). Some

Above: A soldier from the 6th Royal Australian Regiment scrambles up a beach in California on an interoperability exercise in 1989.

of these are increasingly sophisticated, British and US uniform even incorporating anti-reflective dyes to confuse night-vision scopes. Materials such as Gore-Tex, which allows perspiration to evaporate while keeping out rainwater, make advanced jackets for the modern combat soldier, while boots made of similar materials have reduced incidences of age-old maladies such as trench foot. Load-carrying systems are now no longer based purely on belt and straps. For example, the US Army's Integrated Individual Fighting System places most of its pouches on the back and front of a close-fitting vest, keeping weight more aligned over the body's centre of gravity.

The economics of the modern world has meant that armies have become smaller and smaller in many countries, but operational demands mean that each soldier receives more per capita in terms of equipment than those of 50 years ago. Add to that the fear of public response to casualties in conflict, a primary political fear following the Vietnam War, and investment is made in the world's wealthier countries to give each soldier the best survival chance possible. Hence the future will have uniforms with camouflages which change with the terrain; helmets with built-in computer screens for urban combat; materials that enable one uniform to be worn regardless of climate. Looking into the twenty-first century, survivability has become the guiding consideration in how uniforms are designed and produced.

Private Abyssinian Patriot Army Ethiopia 1941

Abyssinia fell under Italian control in 1935 after an invasion from the Italian territories of Somaliland and Eritrea. With the onset of World War II, the Italians thus used Abyssinia as a jumping-off point for their East African campaigns into the Sudan and Kenya. However, resistance from Abyssinian patriots and an effective British campaign in the region returned Abyssinia to its own control in May 1941. The soldier pictured here is one of the Abyssinian resistance fighters who fought alongside the Allies. There was no uniform as such, the patriots usually utilizing whatever items of European clothing were available. This soldier has a khaki tunic and pantaloons, probably of pre-war Italian or German origin, worn with canvas leggings, but no boots. The rifle is the German 7.62mm (0.3in) 98K, and a pistol hangs from his leather belt.

Date:	1941
Unit:	Abyssinian Patriot Army
Rank:	Private
Theatre:	Africa
Location:	Ethiopia

Private
Afghan Army
Afghanistan 1980

As this soldier demonstrates, the troops of the Afghan Army were ill equipped to fight the highly motivated Mujahedeen guerrillas during the Soviet Union's 10-year occupation of Afghanistan. The standard grey-drab combat uniform and soft-peaked cap provided scant protection from the severe Afghan weather, and gave a poor appearance on the parade ground (it doubled as parade kit). The webbing is of local manufacture from cheap leather, and the civilian belt has an inadvisably shiny gold buckle which could be an aiming point for a sniper. The rifle is the venerable Mosin-Nagant 7.62mm (0.3in) M1944 carbine, a weapon with origins back in 1898 and, by 1980, hopelessly outdated against the AK series rifles. Canvas gaiters, worn to protect against mud and water intrusion, feature stud-reinforced black leather sections. Afghan soldiers were inconsistently equipped throughout the conflict.

Date:	1980
Unit:	Afghan Army
Rank:	Private
Location:	Afghan mountains
Conflict:	Afghan War

15

Guerrilla Fighter Mujahedeen Afghanistan 1980

As is typical of guerrilla fighters the world over, dress often tends to be civilian for both reasons of availability and the tactical advantages of an anonymous appearance. Here the jacket and calf-length trousers are made from local cloth, and the sandals from riveted leather, both to traditional designs. More ceremonial elements of dress include the traditional head-dress and the blue sash wrapped around the upper body. No webbing is worn, and all supplies are carried in the musette bag hung over one shoulder. The weapon is a bolt-action hunting rifle, but as the war progressed the guerrillas were often seen with more advanced arms, either captured from the Soviets or US-supplied (mainly AK rifles) being shipped over the Pakistan/Afghan border. The Mujahedeen did an effective job of battling the Soviet occupation and destroying morale amongst the occupying troops.

Date:	1980
Unit:	Mujahedeen
Rank:	Guerrilla Fighter
Location:	Afghan mountains
Conflict:	Afghan War

Guerrilla
Algerian National
Liberation Army
Algeria 1960

Though the revolutionary soldiers of the *Armée de Libéracion Nationale* (ALN) equipped themselves from many sources, they did attain some level of formalized appearance through Soviet kit, weapons and equipment delivered through Egypt. Yet this only took effect from 1959, and the ALN's attempts to oust the French Government from Algeria began as far back as 1954, when the uniform tended towards US supplies retained from World War II. This soldier has several items of US source. His jacket is from the US M1943 uniform and his rifle is the US M2 carbine, a .30 calibre weapon with a short range but a full-automatic capability, which distinguished it from its semi-auto predecessor, the M1. However, the trousers and the cap are French, captured from French forces during action, and the suede boots are civilian.

Date:	1960
Unit:	Algerian National Liberation Army
Rank:	Guerrilla Fighter
Location:	Tunisian/Algerian border
Conflict:	Algerian Independence War

Mercenary
FNLA
Angola 1975

The *Frente Nacional de Libertao de Angola* (FNLA) became a repository for many mercenaries from around the world during its struggles for Angola's independence from Portugal. This mercenary is fairly nondescript in appearance; there is certainly nothing to give an indication of his native country. He wears a ubiquitous olive-drab uniform, probably of African origin, and a peaked cap with neck protector to give the necessary resistance to heat exhaustion and sunburn. His weapon is the Soviet AKM rifle. The AKM, an improved and modernized version of the AK-47, entered production in the 1950s, and can be identified from the original Kalashnikov by the lozenge-shaped indentation above the magazine housing. The Soviet Union pumped thousands of them into the many Cold War bush conflicts which riddled Africa in the 1960s and 1970s, and many are still in use today.

Date:	1975
Unit:	FNLA
Rank:	Mercenary
Location:	Angola
Conflict:	Angolan Independence War

Senior Sergeant Argentine Marines East Falkland 1982

During the Falklands War in 1980, the arctic conditions of the South Atlantic posed a challenge to British and Argentine forces alike. Though standards of uniform wavered throughout the Argentine Army, this NCO has good clothing for the environment (the Argentine Marines tended to receive a higher quality of winter uniform than regular units). He wears a thermal parka jacket: padded, windproof and waterproof, with a deep hood capable of going over the helmet. The helmet is of US supply, as is the webbing and ammunition pouches on the belt (more ammunition is carried in the two bandoliers hung over the shoulders). As the US was a major supplier of military stock to Argentina, a US Army appearance is typical amongst its forces, but the blue-and-white patch above the red rank chevrons on the chest clearly defines nationality. The soldier carries eye goggles for protection against the weather.

Date:	1982
Unit:	Argentine Marines
Rank:	Senior Sergeant
Location:	East Falkland
Conflict:	Falklands War

Marine Buzo Tactico Commandos Falklands 1982

The Argentine Marines' own special forces unit – the Buzo Tactico – played an active part in the Falklands War, particularly in the initial invasion and the capture of Port Stanley. Yet the rest of their war was inauspicious; the unit suffered significant casualties and was outperformed by British forces. Like all special-forces units, its soldiers had the best uniforms and equipment of their nation, usually hand selected by the soldiers. Much of this trooper's uniform is not military at all – the quilted jacket and trousers are civilian mountaineering wear – though the woollen hat is traditionally worn by Argentine special forces as a signature item. The weapon is the British L34A1, a suppressed version of the Sterling submachine gun; magazines, stored in a leather pouch on the hip, are next to a 9mm Browning pistol.

Date:	April 1982
Unit:	Buzo Tactico
Rank:	Marine
Location:	Port Stanley
Conflict:	Falklands War

Corporal Australian Infantry Gallipoli 1915

British Commonwealth casualties at Gallipoli during the period from February 1915 to January 1916 numbered 213,980. This was a hideous cost for an operation that had little strategic effect on the development of World War I. Many of the causalities were sustained by Australian forces, and battles for Turkish positions such as Lone Pine – in which the Australians lost 1700 men alone – are legendary in Australian military history. This soldier wears the standard service dress: a single-breasted khaki tunic in a British pattern, corduroy trousers (though khaki trousers of the same material as the tunic were also worn), puttees and brown leather shoes. A leather belt around the waist supports two pouches, each with ammunition for the .303in (7.7mm) SMLE Mk III Rifle, here fitted with pattern sword bayonet with curved quillon. The distinctive Australian touch is added by the wide-brimmed slouch hat.

Date:	1915
Unit:	Australian Infantry
Rank:	Corporal
Theatre:	South-east Europe
Location:	Gallipoli

Private 6th Division Australian Army North Africa 1941

The uniform here is representative of Australian infantry clothing not only of the time, but also the 20 years which preceded it. The defining item is the headgear: the traditional wide-brimmed felt slouch hat, with the left side fastened up by a regimental badge when worn formally. The tunic had a distinctive design: four pockets to the front, four bronzed buttons as the main shirt fastening, a sectioned cuff and a unit insignia worn on the collar and sleeve (the soldier here has a formation sign on his sleeve which differs from the World War I version by having a grey border). This soldier is typical of Australian infantry in wearing canvas anklets. The 6th Division was heavily involved in North African campaigns of early 1941, and this soldier shows the kit of early deployment, including Lee Enfield rifle, 1908-pattern webbing and 1907-pattern sword bayonet.

Date	January 1941
Unit	6th Division, Australian Army
Rank	Private
Theatre	Mediterranean
Location	North Africa

Private
7th Division
Australian Army
Syria 1941

This Australian infantryman of the 7th Division wears the typical khaki drill uniform of the British infantry in the same theatre. The webbing is the 1937-pattern, here featuring only two utility/ammunition pouches strapped to the belt with a scabbard for the 1899 sword bayonet, here seen attached to his Short Magazine Lee Enfield (SMLE) rifle. This bayonet had some utility in the open spaces of the deserts of North Africa, yet in other theatres its excessive length was a liability, and it was replaced by a shortened version to accompany the No. 4 Mk I rifle. As seen in earlier illustrations, two particular items of dress set him apart as an Australian soldier: the felt slouch hat and the canvas anklets. The wide-brimmed slouch hat would have been a much more welcome form of desert headgear than the traditional British Mk 1 helmet.

Date	March 1941
Unit	7th Division, Australian Army
Rank	Private
Theatre	Mediterranean
Location	Syria

Private 9th Division Australian Army Tobruk 1941

Though the native Australian infantry uniform was actually more suited to desert conditions because of its lighter material, British Army uniforms steadily became the norm as the North African campaign progressed. This soldier reflects those changes. His uniform is entirely British, apart from the canvas anklets. He wears the British infantry's Mk 1 helmet (with goggles to protect his eyes against flying sand and sun glare) with a British single-breasted greatcoat over a khaki desert/tropical uniform. He is heavily encumbered by a British 1937-pattern webbing system, on which hang two bulky utility pouches. Ammunition seems to be this soldier's priority, as he carries additional rounds in a cloth bandolier, while general supplies are stocked in the khaki pouch on his chest. The rifle he carries is the Lee Enfield No.1 Mk III.

Date	May 1941
Unit	9th Division, Australian Army
Rank	Private
Theatre	Mediterranean
Location	Tobruk

Private
9th Division
Australian Army
Tobruk 1941

The 9th Division of the Australian Army paid a heavy price during the fighting of 1941–42 in North Africa. Total casualties or soldiers lost as POWs numbered over 6000, enormous losses for a division-size unit. The Australian Army suffered some 19,351 losses throughout the war in actions against German forces (including 3552 dead), yet against the Japanese the toll would be greater: 42,224 with over 15,000 killed. Considering that the Australian Army began the war with just over 82,000 men, the scale of Australia's sacrifice becomes clear. This soldier is one of the three Australian Army divisions – the 6th, 7th and 9th – deployed to North Africa in 1941. The kit and uniform is almost entirely British: Mk 1 helmet, 1937 webbing, Lee Enfield rifle. One notable item is the leather jerkin, which provided protection against low desert temperatures.

Date	October 1941
Unit	9th Division, Australian Army
Rank	Private
Theatre	Mediterranean
Location	Tobruk

Leading Seaman Royal Australian Navy Sydney 1943

This sailor belongs to Task Force 44, a contingent of the Royal Australian Navy which took part in the Allied attempts to recapture the Philippines. The similarity of appearance between this man and a Royal Navy rating is not coincidental; the navy whites of the Royal Navy on Pacific duties also served as the standard RAN uniform (both forces also shared a serge temperate uniform). The distinction between the two lies in the detail. The cap is scripted with 'HMAS' of the Australian Navy and the buttons of the jacket were marked with Australian references. This sailor's rank is shown by the anchor on his sleeve, while the chevron is a merit badge for three years or more of good conduct. The badge on his right sleeve indicates his status as a leading torpedo man. The RAN served throughout the Pacific region and the Mediterranean.

Date:	May 1943
Unit:	Task Force 44, RAN
Rank:	Leading Seaman
Theatre:	Pacific
Location:	Sydney

Trooper
AATTV
Vietnam 1970

Australia's contribution to the Vietnam War was comparatively small, but significant. Its Special Forces contingent was in large measure supplied by the Australian SAS and the AATTV (Australian Army Training Team Vietnam). Only around 100 men strong, the AATTV conducted numerous combat and 'hearts and minds' missions, which resulted in four Victoria Crosses for bravery. This soldier, on a jungle patrol, wears the 'Tigerstripe' pattern of camouflage, which became a virtual signature of Allied Special Forces during the war. His kit signifies the likelihood of combat. He carries a powerful 7.62mm (0.3in) SLR weapon with two ammunition pouches on his belt – part of a US M56 webbing system – two M8 smoke-grenades, and a satchel which would often contain plastic explosive or Claymore mines. Most of his kit is of foreign origin, but his boots are Australian kangaroo hide, durable footwear for the humid environment.

Date:	1970
Unit:	Australian Army Training Team Vietnam
Rank:	Trooper
Location:	Vietnamese Highlands, South Vietnam
Conflict:	Vietnam War

Trooper Australian SAS Philippines 1980s

The Australian SAS matches the qualities of its British counterpart, and forms the vanguard of Australian Special Forces. It has acquired a significant operational record since formation in 1957. From service alongside the British SAS in Brunei in the 1960s, it went on to serve with distinction in the Vietnam War, and in recent years has engaged in aggressive peacekeeping actions in East Timor. Its uniforms revolve around the environments most likely to be faced in the Oceanic/Pacific region, jungle and outback. As élite troops, they get to hand-pick their kit. This soldier is ideally dressed for jungle operations, with camouflaged combat suit and a sweat-rag, as helmets tend to snag on branches. The rifle is the M16A1, a rifle proven in the jungles of Vietnam, but which needs diligent cleaning to maintain its reliability.

Date	1980s
Unit	Australian SAS
Rank:	Trooper
Location:	Philippines
Conflict:	Training

Private Austro-Hungarian Army Serbia 1914

The uniform of the Austro-Hungarian forces was established in its basic form in 1909. During this year a new uniform in pike-grey – known as a *Hechtgrau* – was introduced to all infantry units, including the artillery, Mounted Tyrolean and Dalmatian rifles (not, however, to cavalry regiments). The tunic was single-breasted with a stand collar (though later a stand-and-fall collar) and was made in wool for winter and drill for summer. Foot soldiers wore long trousers with an integral gaiter buttoned at the ankle, though here this soldier wears conventional puttees. Headgear varied considerably, including a black kepi for many infantry officers, side caps and, as here, a cloth peaked service cap. German steel helmets were worn from 1915, mainly by assault troops. This man's rifle is the 8mm (0.31in) Mannlicher Model 1895.

Date:	1914
Unit:	Austro-Hungarian Infantry
Rank:	Private
Theatre:	Southern Europe
Location:	Serbia

Officer
Austrian Hussars
Serbia 1914

World War I saw the end of the credibility of horse-mounted cavalry. For many nations this lesson died hard, especially true in the Austro-Hungarian Army, as Hungary was the home of the hussar. We see from this hussar officer how tradition left a uniform unsuited to the realities of mechanized warfare. The bright blue Attila jacket (here with gold braiding for an officer; other ranks wore red) and red trousers presented a clear sight picture to snipers and machine gunners alike. Before the war, hussars wore the elaborate shako helmet, but after 1914, a peaked field cap with grey cover. The tunic was often worn slung over the left shoulder like a pelisse. This hussar also carries his cutlass on his left hip, though he is actually using a more modern form of weapon, a 9mm Roth-Steyr M1912 pistol. The hideous losses amongst the hussars led to the adoption of standard grey infantry uniforms during 1915.

Date:	1914
Unit:	Austrian Hussars
Rank:	Officer
Theatre:	Southern Europe
Location:	Serbia

Guerrilla Fighter Bangladesh Liberation Army East Pakistan 1971

The creation of the state of Bangladesh was one of the bloodiest episodes in recent Indian history. The *Mukti Bahini* (Bangladesh Liberation Army) was amongst several guerrilla forces in East Pakistan attempting – ultimately successfully – to wrest their region from the control of West Pakistan. The guerrilla here is lightly dressed but powerfully armed (the guerrillas were materially supported by the Indian Army, which eventually invaded East Pakistan to force the establishment of the independent Bangladesh). Clothing is civilian, though this man has made an ammunition bandolier. His helmet is of British Army origin, but its lines are obscured by camouflage. The machine gun is the German MG3, an updated version of the MG42, which gave such violent service in World War II and was noted for its fast rate of fire.

Date:	1971
Unit:	Bangladesh Liberation Army
Rank:	Guerrilla Fighter
Location:	East Pakistan
Conflict:	East Pakistan Independence War

Colonel
1st Infantry Regiment
Belgian Army
Belgium 1940

Belgian military uniform in the early years of the war followed a French pattern for the private soldiers and NCOs, but adopted British-style uniforms for the officers. This colonel of the 1st Infantry Regiment illustrates this division of styles. Working from the top, we find a British Army-style peaked service cap. The crown in the centre of the cap indicates the arm-of-service, not by the motif but by the colour (each arm had its own service colour). This cap would come with different chin cords: gold for officers, silver for warrant officers, and a brown strap for lower ranks. Beneath the officer's thigh-length tunic, a white or light khaki shirt was worn with a khaki tie. On the lower half of the body, Belgian officers tended to wear trousers in beige cord or khaki. Footwear could be a pair of brown shoes or a pair of knee-length riding boots.

Date:	April 1940
Unit:	1st Infantry Regiment
Rank:	Colonel
Theatre:	North-west Europe
Location:	Belgium

Sergeant
Infantry Division
Belgian Army
Belgium 1940

This NCO demonstrates the French style of private- and NCO-rank uniforms in the Belgian Army. The steel helmet is a direct French copy, though with a Belgian lion's head on the front (a painted regimental number and crown was an alternative). He wears a single breasted jacket with stand-and-fall collar, with an infantry crown on the shoulder-straps and regimental number and rank displayed on the sleeve. His webbing is standard Belgian issue, showing six small pouches with ammunition for his 7.65mm (0.301in) Mauser M1889 rifle. Belgian infantry distinguished their arm-of-service through the helmet and jacket. Motorized troops had a special leather-covered helmet and a short, brown leather coat. Rifle soldiers wore a black leather coat or single-breasted greatcoat and a green beret with boar's head cap badge.

Date:	May 1940
Unit:	Belgian Army
Rank:	Sergeant
Theatre:	North-west Europe
Location:	Belgium

Major
1st Regiment
Belgian Air Force
Belgium 1940

May 1940 was a dark time for all Belgian forces, not least the air force. Of 250 aircraft available, only 50 were modern. The Belgian pilots fought bravely, but against the Luftwaffe they had little chance of operational impact. As with Belgian Army officers, Belgian Air Force officers tended towards an English cut in the style of their uniforms. This Major wears a blue-grey uniform of Royal Air Force type, though the forage cap and riding boots set him apart from that unit (Belgian personnel who did serve with the RAF had a light-blue shoulder flash on a dark-blue or grey background to distinguish their nationality). Air force membership is made evident through the aviator's badge on the cap – which has a black band for officers – and the sleeve. Ground personnel and NCOs wore a propeller badge on the cap and shoulder-straps.

Date:	May 1940
Unit:	1st Regiment, Belgian Air Force
Rank:	Major
Theatre:	North-west Europe
Conflict::	Belgium

Warrant Officer Belgian Paracommando Regiment Congo 1964

The Belgian Paracommando Regiment gained public prominence in the Congolese Civil War in 1964, when it liberated 2000 hostages from anti-government rebels in a US-assisted parachute operation near Stanleyville, where this soldier is pictured. From the 1st Battalion, he bears a strong visual allegiance to the British Parachute Regiment which inspired the Belgian unit. He wears the paras' maroon beret, whose SAS badge refers to the first Belgian para company which conducted operations with the SAS in World War II. His jacket is a Belgian version of the British paras' Denison smock, and his rank is displayed on red slides on the shoulder-straps (the star is the rank, the red the regimental colours). Ammunition for his 7.62mm (0.3in) FN FAL rifle is stored on his British 1937-pattern web belt.

Date:	1964
Unit:	1st Battalion, Belgian Paracommando Regiment
Rank:	Warrant Officer
Location:	Stanleyville, Congo
Conflict:	Congolese Civil War

NCO
Belgian
Parachute Regiment
Belgium 1990s

This modern Belgian para shares his appearance with many modern European armies. His uniform is in a Woodland pattern similar to British Army Disruptive Pattern Material (DPM), though in Belgium this pattern actually separates the paras from the rest of the army, who wear a plain olive-drab. Unlike the 1st and 3rd Battalions of the paras, who wear the classic red beret, the 2nd Battalion (to which this soldier belongs) wears the green beret. This alludes to their involvement with British commando forces during World War II. In action or training, the beret is generally replaced by a NATO ballistic nylon helmet with double chin-strap (the double strap gives better fit during parachute jumps). The weapon held here is the 7.62mm (0.3in) FN MAG machine gun, a Belgian weapon which has claim to being one of the best machine guns of the last century.

Date:	1990s
Unit:	2nd Battalion, Belgian Parachute Regiment
Rank:	NCO
Location:	Belgium
Conflict:	None

Private
Biafran Army
East Nigeria 1968

The Biafran Army fought an independence war for three years (1967–70) against the much more powerful and well-equipped Nigerian Army. Though they performed well as individuals, the Biafrans suffered from a chronic lack of materiel, and took military supplies from a range of sources, both military and civilian, a situation evident in the soldier here. His shirt and jacket are unknown, though probably taken from the Soviet-supplied kit which flooded many countries of Africa during the Cold War period. The wellington boots are civilian, hardly suitable or comfortable footwear for the African heat. He wears a soft cap, though Biafran soldiers can be seen in a variety of US and Soviet helmets during the conflict. For armament, a 7.62mm (0.3in) Vz58 assault rifle is carried – a Czech copy of the Kalashnikov AK47 – and a single large ammunition pouch for the 30-round magazines is strapped on his left hip.

Date:	1968
Unit:	Biafran Army
Rank:	Private
Location:	East Nigeria
Conflict:	Biafran Independence War

37

Guerrilla Khmer Rouge Cambodia 1975

The leadership and soldiers of Pol Pot's Khmer Rouge inflicted one of the worst genocides in twentieth-century history within Cambodia, renamed Kampuchea after the Khmer Rouge take-over in 1975. Being a guerrilla army, the Khmer Rouge had some diversity of dress and kit, yet there were essentially two patterns of recognizable uniform. The first was a formal olive-green or dark-brown military uniform which was sourced from the Khmer Rouge's main Communist suppliers, China and North Vietnam. This soldier wears a Chinese Liberation Army cap, yet the rest of his appearance is perhaps more common of the Khmer Rouge. The jacket and trousers are civilian working clothes, following the Khmer Rouge's proletarian philosophy, while the neckscarf (often red and white) was Khmer Rouge identification. This soldier, armed with a Type 56 assault rifle, has ammunition in 'ChiCom' (Chinese Communist) chest pouches.

Date:	1975
Unit:	Khmer Rouge
Rank:	Guerrilla Fighter
Location:	Rural Cambodia
Conflict:	Cambodian Civil War

Lieutenant
Royal Canadian
Women's Naval Service
London 1943

Female personnel in the Royal Canadian Navy tended to perform essential shore and administrative duties, which allowed the maximum numbers of men for active service. Hence this lieutenant belongs to the paymaster section, a department identified by the white sections set into the rank lace on the shoulder-straps. This lieutenant's uniform matches that of British ranks except, like many units of the British Empire, in the button details and hat ribbons which illustrated the country of origin. She wears a standard lightweight uniform which was shared with other ranks, but the three-cornered hat separates her as an officer from the round sailor's hat worn by NCOs and lower ranks. The buttons on her jacket are gilt brass instead of the plastic buttons of ratings. She carries a naval-issue bag, called a pouchette, and white gloves.

Date:	June 1943
Unit:	Royal Canadian Women's Naval Service
Rank:	Lieutenant
Theatre:	North-west Europe
Location:	London

Private
Le Regiment de Levis
Canadian Army
England 1944

This soldier was part of the Allied build-up in England in preparation for the D-Day landings on 6 June 1944. His general uniform would have been a close match for British soldiers, but the 'Canada' badge on his upper sleeve leaves no doubt as to his provenance. There are further distinctions; the cap is Canadian-pattern, with earflaps (a fur-earflapped version was also produced called the 'Yukon') and has the regimental badge on the front, though as the war progressed, British-style helmets became the norm. The uniform colour was greener than the British, while the cloth was of a better standard. While only officers in the British Army were allowed to wear this style of greatcoat, it was standard kit for Canadian privates and NCOs, an allowance which was due, no doubt, to the bitter cold winter climate of Canada.

Date:	January 1944
Unit:	Le Regiment de Levis
Rank:	Private
Theatre:	North-west Europe
Location:	England

Warrant Officer Princess Patricia's Light Infantry Cyprus 1970s

For the early part of the post-war period, Canada followed the British Army models of kit and dress. However, the Canadian military soon began to forge its own identity, and leaned more on the United States. This soldier of the Princess Patricia's Light Infantry – one of Canada's most prestigious units, formed in 1914 – is at an interesting juncture. His weapon is the British Army's L1A1 Self-Loading Rifle, and his uniform standard Canadian olive-drab. The webbing is based on the US ALICE system, worn with two ammunition/utility pouches. Since then, most forms of kit have become indigenous. The L1A1 was replaced by the C7, a Canadian adaptation of the US M16 rifle, while the latest Improved Environmental Clothing System (IECS), Load Carriage System and Tactical Vest form a superb, home-grown battlefield kit.

Date:	1970s
Unit:	Princess Patricia's Light Infantry
Rank:	Warrant Officer
Location:	Cyprus
Conflict:	Peacekeeping, Cyprus

Crewman
Chadian National Army
Chad 1970

With its independence from France in 1960, Chad suffered a number of civil wars with various anti-government guerrilla factions. Chad's Army was, and is, a rather incoherent organization, split by tendencies towards infighting and also by inconsistencies in weaponry and equipment. This soldier is most likely the crewman of a French Panhard AML-60 or ALM-90 armoured car, the armoured mainstay of the post-independence Chadian Army. He wears French AFV communication headphones, and his paratrooper's shirt and suede boots are also of French origin. However, the bayonet belongs to a Type 56 assault rifle, the Chinese copy of Kalashnikov's infamous AK-47, distributed in large numbers throughout Africa and South-east Asia. Apart from French and Chinese influences, US and Soviet kit was also seen in the Chadian Army.

Date:	1970
Unit:	Chadian National Army
Rank:	Crewman
Location:	Central Chad
Conflict:	Chadian Civil War

1st Lieutenant Chinese Nationalist Air Force China 1939

Because of materiel shortages, and despite large-scale US assistance, wartime Chinese Nationalist Air Force personnel were seen in a variety of dress. This pilot is a 1st Lieutenant, the rank indicated by the eagle and bars on the cuffs (later in the war the rank badges were moved up to the shoulder). Predominantly, like the 1st Lieutenant here, the pilots and ground crew simply wore the khaki tunic and trousers of the army, the main difference being the peaked cap and the insignia. The cap itself featured a light khaki band, a badge showing gold-embroidered wings with an enamel sun-and-sky badge in the centre, and a black leather peak and chin-strap. Similar insignia was also available for a side cap, an alternative for air force personnel. When flying, the Chinese pilots would wear US flying jackets and helmets, or captured Japanese flying gear.

Date:	September 1939
Unit:	Chinese Nationalist Air Force
Rank:	1st Lieutenant
Theatre:	East Asia
Location:	China

Colonel Chinese Nationalist Army China 1942

The Chinese Nationalist Army uniform varied depending on the region of China and the economic and military resources of that region, but essentially the uniform fell into two categories. For winter clothing, the uniform was made in a bright-blue cotton (a rather questionable choice of colour). For summer – as in the case of this army colonel here – the uniform was made of khaki cotton. The tunic was single-breasted with four large front- and side patch pockets and a stand-and-fall collar. Rank and arm-of-service were denoted on the collar patches; in this case the red background indicates the infantry, while the three stars define the rank. These patches were cloth, metal or plastic, and were detachable. From the waist down, the officer clearly follows European riding dress: his trousers had puttees, over which he wore leather riding boots.

Date:	June 1942
Unit:	Chinese Nationalist Army
Rank:	Colonel
Theatre:	Pacific
Location:	China

1st Lieutenant Guerrilla Chinese Communist Forces China 1945

Mao Tse Tung's Chinese Revolutionary Army was a massive force of over 500,000 combatants, despite its irregular status. Over the four years immediately following World War II, this army imposed steady defeat upon government forces by revolutionary war, until it eventually achieved power in 1949. Kit and uniform for the Communists had three predominant sources: either home-made, captured from the Nationalist soldiers, or war surplus following the Japanese defeat, supplied in bulk from the Soviet Union from 1946. This soldier's rifle – a Japanese 6.5mm (0.255in) 38th Year carbine – belongs to the last category, while the uniform is almost entirely home-made. He wears traditional Chinese peasant clothes, an improvised 'webbing' of cotton or canvas bandoliers, and a grenade holder over his left shoulder.

Date:	1945
Unit:	Chinese Communist Forces
Rank:	Revolutionary Fighter
Location:	Southern China
Conflict:	Chinese Civil War

Private Chinese Communist Army China 1945

This soldier resides at the better-equipped end of the spectrum for Chinese Communist troops in the mid-1940s. His uniform is that of the general Chinese Army, including the distinctive knee-height woollen puttees and the stand-and-fall collar shirt. Two items are notable. The first is the system of ammunition carriage, consisting of a sequence of leather pouches of two lengths. The shorter pouches would store pistol rounds or rifle clips, while the longer would carry submachine gun magazines. His submachine gun is the second interesting feature. The US 9mm United Defense Model 42 was a gun of exceptionally high quality and fairly rare in terms of world-wide distribution. This weapon was probably acquired via US OSS units in the Dutch East Indies, and was always the exception in the Chinese Communist Army's personal arsenal.

Date:	1945
Unit:	Chinese Communist Army
Rank:	Private
Location:	Northern China
Conflict:	Chinese Civil War

Private Chinese Nationalist Army China 1945

In its war against the Communists, Chang Kai Shek's Chinese Nationalist Army had several on-paper advantages. Not the least of these was the fact that post-war, the US began to supply it with copious amounts of weaponry and equipment. In the case of this private, this is immediately clear in his .45in Thompson M1A1 submachine gun, a mass-production version of the infamous Thompson M1928A1 which was in heavy service with US and Allied forces throughout World War II. In terms of uniform, the soldier's dress is of World War II type: a light khaki tunic and trousers (above the rank of private, the collar would feature metal, plastic or cloth rank patches), with knee-high woollen puttees, black shoes, and a peaked forage cap. Insignia is minimal, the only apparent badge being the 'white sun blue sky' badge on the cap.

Date:	1945
Unit:	Chinese Nationalist Army
Rank:	Private
Location:	South China
Conflict:	Chinese Civil War

Private Chinese People's Liberation Army Korea 1951

Only a year into the existence of the new Communist state, Chinese forces were once again in combat, this time assisting Communist North Korea in its attempted take-over of UN-backed South Korea. Over the three years of the Korean War, however, the PLA would lose up to one million men, despite early victories over the United Nations forces. The soldier's dress here gives some indication of the severity of the Korean climate. Arctic conditions could prevail in winter, thus he wears a fully quilted jacket and trousers, though the archaic puttees have remained. The cap is fur-lined, with extensive earflaps to prevent frostbite; his footwear does not suggest as much protection. Ammunition for his Type 88 Hanyang rifle is held in cotton bandoliers across the chest, which was popular in East Asian countries.

Date:	1951
Unit:	Chinese People's Liberation Army
Rank:	Private
Location:	South Korea
Conflict:	Korean War

Guerrilla Cuban Revolutionary Forces Havana 1959

The Cuban Revolutionary Forces suffered from a lack of military supplies during the campaign to overthrow the government of Fulgencio Batista, yet intelligent and persistent tactics often made up for this. North American weapons and clothing were the primary fighting kit. Underneath his civilian jacket – emblazoned with a revolutionary Cuban patch – is a standard US herringbone-twill combat uniform. Worn by US Marines and Army soldiers during the Pacific campaign of World War II and the Korean War, it was hard-wearing and comfortable. The webbing is US-type, but the small ammunition pouches on the belt were for holding five-round clips for the M1 Garand semi-automatic rifle, whereas this revolutionary holds an older Springfield M1903 bolt-action firearm. The patch on his arm and beret are typical of guerrilla fighters.

Date:	1959
Unit:	Cuban Revolutionary Forces
Rank:	Guerrilla Fighter
Location:	Havana, Cuba
Conflict:	Cuban Civil War

Private Cuban Army Angola 1976

Cuban forces were involved in substantial numbers in Angolan affairs from the mid-1970s. Angola's new Marxist government, fresh in its independence from the Portuguese, was locked in a civil war with various factions. The well-armed and trained Cubans made a significant impact on the situation, helping to crush the anti-government rebels. Because of the intense Soviet sponsorship of the Cuban Government and ideology, by this period, Cuban kit is mainly of Russian manufacture. The Soviet 7.62mm (0.3in) AKM assault rifle is seen here, with its innovative bayonet and scabbard: the two components lock together to form a wire-cutter. A magazine pouch for the AK's 30-round magazines is seen just behind the weapon. The steel helmet is also a Soviet infantry type, but the rest of the uniform – a simple set of olive-drab fatigues – although it could have come from anywhere, is most likely of Cuban manufacture.

Date:	1976
Unit:	Cuban Army
Rank:	Private
Location:	Angola
Conflict:	Angolan Civil War

Lance-Sergeant 1st Infantry Division Czechoslovak Army France 1940

The exodus of Czech soldiers from their homeland began immediately after the Munich Agreement of 1938, and France became a major destination for many. In France they initially served with the French Foreign Legion, but actually began to form themselves into Czech units once France had entered the war, primarily the 1st Czech Division. Everything in this lance-sergeant's uniform is of French origin, apart from the insignia. Czech soldiers in France displayed rank on the shoulder-straps, and also wore their officer's graduation badges over the right pocket. Other than these markings, the French influence runs throughout. The tunic, pantaloons and helmet are of French infantry issue. The soldier carries the French 8mm (0.315) M1892 revolver which, though fairly ineffectual, served with French forces until the end of the war.

Date:	May 1940
Unit:	1st Infantry Regiment, Czech Army
Rank:	Lance-Sergeant
Theatre:	North-west Europe
Location:	France

51

Staff Captain Czechoslovak Air Force France 1940

The pilots of the Czech Air Force served bravely in both British and French air forces following the annexation of Czechoslovakia by Germany in 1939. This staff captain is pictured here while stationed in France and, like the Czech infantry in France, has adopted French uniform. The jacket and trousers form the French Louise-Blue uniform, but the insignia and badges mark the man out as a Czech national. On the jacket, the pilot wears a French pilot's badge on the right breast pocket, with aircraft wings above, while on the left pocket he has his Czech pilot's badge (he also has the *Croix de Guerre* medal ribbon). The peaked cap continues the Czech identification, as does the lion and wings centred over the peak. Combatants would also have crossed swords on the badge, omitted for non-combatants. The cap is finished with gold strap cords.

Date:	May 1940
Unit:	Czechoslovak Air Force
Rank:	Staff Captain
Theatre:	North-west Europe
Location:	France

General
Minister of Defence
Czechoslovak Army
England 1940

Depicted here is the Czech Minister of Defence-in-Exile, General Sergej Ingr, seen shortly after his escape from Czechoslovakia to England. Significant numbers of Czech Army soldiers made their way to the UK, and were based, trained and restructured at Cholmondeley Castle, near Chester, before being sent to bases around British cities. The main influences on the Czech uniform were British and French. The strong Czech alliance with France meant that French tunics, helmets and trousers were common; indeed, the General's tunic is of French origin. However, British uniforms became the norm after time spent in the UK, though with Czech badges and a 'Czechoslovakia' title on the upper left sleeve. The General's tunic has the rank denoted on the shoulder-straps, while the three stars on the sleeve indicate divisional commander.

Date:	November 1940
Unit:	Czech Ministry of Defence
Rank:	General
Theatre:	North-west Europe
Location:	England

Private
Jutland Division
Danish Army
Denmark 1940

The Danish Army presented no significant resistance to the German invasion in 1940, and the occupation was on especially lenient terms. The Danes were allowed to retain widespread control over their governmental, legal and administrative affairs, and even kept a small army of just over 3000 men. The reasons behind this can be seen in the uniform and kit of this soldier: smart but utterly dated. Although Denmark had a modern khaki uniform from 1923, it was in store by 1940, and soldiers were kitted out in World War I-pattern clothing. This uniform is the wool 1915-pattern in grey-blue with an M1923 helmet. Rations and personal effects are in the backpack, while the container beneath holds a 1926-pattern gas mask. The black pouch on the belt holds ammunition clips. The bayonet is for the M1889 8mm (0.314in) rifle.

Date:	January 1940
Unit:	Jutland Division
Rank:	Private
Theatre:	Baltic
Location:	Denmark

1st Lieutenant Reconnaissance Unit Danish Air Force Denmark 1940

At the point of German invasion, Denmark had only 50 military aircraft. The Danish Air Force units were further weakened by the fact that they were split between the army and navy, services in rivalry with one another, and thus found it difficult to present a united command. The similarity of this officer to a Danish Army soldier indicates that he falls under the auspices of the army. Air force personnel wore army uniforms for its ground dress, in this case a khaki M1923-pattern uniform, with closed- or open-collar tunics (here the closed collar), trousers flared at the thighs, and knee-high boots. The arm-of-service is indicated by a set of flying wings on the right breast, and the lieutenant's rank is given by the stars on the blue shoulder-straps and the gold star on the collar. When flying, British Royal Air Force jackets and flying helmets were used.

Date:	January 1940
Unit:	Reconnaissance Unit
Rank:	1st Lieutenant
Theatre:	Baltic
Location:	Denmark

Warrant Officer 7th Infantry Regiment Danish Army Denmark 1940

The 1923-pattern uniform which this warrant officer wears is entirely obscured by his heavy black 1864 greatcoat, another dated piece of uniform in Danish use. The greatcoat was double-breasted and featured a stand-and-fall collar plus turn-back cuffs (1923-pattern trousers also featured turn-back ankles on the trousers), with two rows of buttons. The only markings it would usually carry were those denoting rank and arm-of-service. Rank markings were on the shoulder-straps; this soldier has the two gold rosettes on the brown, silk shoulder- straps of a warrant officer. Arm-of-service badges were worn on the coat or tunic collar. Completing the soldier's uniform are black, pull-on boots and the awkward-looking Danish steel helmet. A khaki field cap – an alternative form of headgear – is tucked into his Sam Browne belt.

Date:	February 1940
Unit:	7th Infantry Regiment
Rank:	Warrant Officer
Theatre:	Baltic
Location:	Denmark

Guerrilla
Dhofari
Guerrilla Forces
Oman 1973

From 1965 to 1974, nationalist guerrillas of the Dhofar province, Oman, began an armed struggle for independence against the forces of the ruling Sultan. The guerrillas would grow in number throughout this period, but in 1975 were finally defeated by Omani military strength and their own internal factionalism. Support for their cause came mainly from the Soviet Union, and thus Communist items of kit, uniform and weaponry are common. This fighter is dressed in the traditional civilian skirt and head-dress, supplemented by supplies from the Soviet Union and Eastern Bloc. His weapon is the 7.62mm (0.3in) AKM, the modernized version of Kalashnikov's AK-47. His East German jacket, here in a leaf-pattern camouflage, was developed for use by élite German units in World War II. Webbing is British 1958-pattern fitted with an AKM pouch.

Date:	1973
Unit:	Dhofari Guerrilla Forces
Rank:	Guerrilla
Location:	Dhofar
Conflict:	Omani Civil War

Private
Egyptian Army
Southern Israel 1948

This soldier is seen at a pivotal moment in Middle Eastern history: when the combined forces of several Arab states, including Egypt, Iraq and Syria, attacked the one-day-old Jewish State of Israel. The outcome of the conflict in Israel's favour has repercussions to this day. This soldier's webbing, boots and weaponry allude clearly to Egypt's close links with the United Kingdom at this time. The rifle is the British .303in (7.7mm) Short Magazine Lee Enfield Mk III, here fitted with a 1907-pattern bayonet. Ammunition is carried in the 1937-pattern webbing, still standard British issue at this time for non-tropical operations. The boots and garters are also British issue. The uniform itself is of Egyptian manufacture, a simple khaki denim one-piece overall, fly-fronted, and with a standing collar and matching beret (cavalry, military police and artillery soldiers wore green, red and black caps respectively).

Date:	1948
Unit:	Egyptian Army
Rank:	Private
Location:	Southern Israel
Conflict:	Israeli War of Independence

Private
Egyptian Army
Commandos
Sinai 1967

By 1967, during which year Israel launched the lightning Six-Day War on its immediate Arab neighbours, Cold War sponsorship of the conflict in the Middle East had broadly settled into Soviet backing for the Arab armies, and Western backing for Israel. Though this Egyptian soldier is mostly kitted out with local uniform and equipment, the Soviet influence is seen in the Russian infantryman's helmet and also the gas-mask pack which can just be seen on the left hip. The other item on the belt is actually an aberration – a US water bottle in an M1941 cover – one which illustrates that many Arab soldiers had to innovate in how they put together their kit. The uniform is an Egyptian-made desert-camouflage tunic and trousers. The weapon is the Egyptian Port Said submachine gun, a copy of the Swedish 9mm Carl Gustav, made under licence in Egypt.

Date:	1967
Unit:	Egyptian Army Commandos
Rank:	Private
Location:	Sinai
Conflict:	Six-Day War

Private Egyptian Army Sinai 1967

While commandos and élite regiments of the Egyptian armed forces tended to wear camouflage uniforms, the standard uniform of the Egyptian infantryman was as depicted here. The plain khaki denim overall was hard-wearing, if giving little temperature control in the desert. This soldier carries a blanket around his shoulders for the desert nights when the temperatures can drop precipitously. Soviet kit is again in evidence. The AK rifle is seen here with its bayonet fitted, and the soldier's headgear is the Soviet infantry helmet used by all Egyptian ground forces at the time. He has no webbing system as such, just a civilian leather belt fitted with water bottle and a Soviet-issue haversack slung over his shoulder for various rations and utility items. An interesting reference to the UK lies in the British 1937-pattern web anklets, which were probably left over from World War II occupation.

Date:	1967
Unit:	Egyptian Army
Rank:	Private
Location:	Sinai
Conflict:	Six-Day War

Crewman
Egyptian
Armed Forces
Sinai 1973

The 1973 Yom Kippur War between Israel and Egypt and Syria actually featured one of the greatest tank battles of the twentieth century, fought between some 2000 main battle tanks in the Sinai desert. The Arab forces used Soviet T54/55 tanks; the Israelis British Centurions and US M47/48 Pattons. This Egyptian crewman wears a simple cotton khaki overall of Egyptian 1955-issue pattern. His headgear, of Soviet origin, features an internal headset for receiving radio communications, and over his left shoulder hangs the throat microphone which he would use on the move. The other lead is for the RT/IC internal communications radio. The padded helmet must have been uncomfortable to wear in the desert, as the fur lining indicates a winter issue. The future of this tankman is not known: Israeli armour inflicted a huge defeat on the Egyptian tanks.

Date:	1973
Unit:	Egyptian Armoured Force
Rank:	Crewman
Location:	West Sinai
Conflict:	Yom Kippur War

Private
Salvadorian Army
El Salvador 1980

The Salvadorian Army is actually one of the most professional in the whole of Latin America, with high standards of training and discipline. It is also a battle-tested force, fighting in El Salvador's long-running civil wars from the 1970s to the 1990s. During this period, the army received heavy amounts of US materiel support, to which this soldier is testimony. The entire uniform is US produced, the shirt and trousers being simple olive-drab fatigues, while the helmet is the vintage M1 steel helmet. The boots are made from a nylon-and-leather mix, a type of boot developed for US forces in the tropical conditions of Vietnam. Webbing is the US M1943 pattern with an M1956 belt. An emphatic departure from US kit, however, is the German rifle, a 7.62mm (0.3in) Heckler & Koch G3A3. It has had amazing export success in over 60 countries, South America being one of its biggest markets.

Date:	1980
Unit:	Salvadorian Army
Rank:	Private
Location:	El Salvador
Conflict:	El Salvador Civil War

Guerrilla
Eritrean
Liberation Front
Eritrea 1979

War between Ethiopia and Eritrea lasted from 1962 – when Ethiopia forcibly annexed Eritrea – to 1993 when Eritrea finally regained independence. The main resistance body within Eritrea was the Eritrean Liberation Front. Though chronically under-resourced, the ELF managed to provide a fairly determined foe for the Ethiopian Army. This ELF fighter is dressed as many of his force were: with anything they could acquire. An approach at a standard uniform was made in the form of a khaki tunic and trousers, but this was never consistent through the entire force. This soldier is mostly wearing civilian clothing: denim shirt, cotton trousers, plimsolls and headscarf. However, he has managed to acquire a British 1937-pattern web belt and ammunition pouch, the pouch used to store magazines for his Czech Cz58 assault rifle, which fired M1943 rounds.

Date:	1979
Unit:	Eritrean Liberation Front
Rank:	Guerrilla Fighter
Location:	Eritrea
Conflict:	Eritrean Independence War

Seaman
Lake Lagoda Flotilla
Finnish Navy
Lake Lagoda 1939

This Finnish sailor is amply dressed for the severe weather conditions of the Baltic. His two-piece fleece-lined foul-weather suit with fur collar would give good protection against arctic winds, rains and ice storms. Underneath he would be wearing the standard 'square rig' uniform of the Finnish Navy. This consisted of a double-breasted blue jacket with an open left breast pocket and two flapped side pockets, this being worn in combination with a white shirt and black tie, blue trousers and black shoes. The cap worn here, featuring a circular cockade of the national colours, is the standard naval headgear, and the word across the front would indicate either the ship or the installation (the Finnish Navy also ran coastal artillery). Officers were distinguished by a dark-blue peaked cap, the rank indicated on the cuffs, greatcoat and tunic shoulder-straps.

Date:	September 1939
Unit:	Lake Lagoda Flotilla
Rank:	Seaman
Theatre:	Baltic
Location:	Lake Lagoda

Marshal Mannerheim Finnish Army Helsinki 1939

Marshal Mannerheim was the head of the very small (nine divisions) but resilient Finnish Army. However, this army would suffer greatly in the war, when some 89,000 Finnish military personnel were killed. Mannerheim was exclusive in his title of Marshal, and so his uniform must be treated in many ways as unique to his person. With his plain field-grey tunic and riding trousers, he wears a singularly unostentatious display of his rank and merits. Around his neck he wears the Mannerheim Cross of the Cross of Liberty for bravery, while decorations ribbons are placed over his left breast. His shoulder-straps feature the regimental insignia of Mannerheim's former regiment, the Uusimaa dragoons, and silver Finnish lions. He wears no rank badges – three gold lions with crossed batons on a silver background – but there is a Civil Guard badge on his left sleeve.

Date:	September 1939
Unit:	Finnish Army
Rank:	Marshal
Theatre:	Eastern Front
Location:	Helsinki

Captain
2nd Division
Finnish Army
Leningrad 1943

This Captain wears a dark-grey Model 1936 uniform, the standard uniform of the Finnish Army which resulted from a modernization of the old light-grey uniform in that year. Subtle distinctions of cloth quality, style and insignia separated the officers from the lower ranks. The standard tunic was single-breasted with four patch pockets and a stand-and-fall collar. Matching breeches were issued, this officer's being reinforced with leather sections – the Finnish Army had a strong cavalry tradition – and a pair of knee-high boots in brown leather. The winter field cap was worn by all soldiers, the officers' with a gilt-metal lion badge above the central buttons, while the lower ranks wore the Finnish blue-and-white cockade. Also issued were the German 1935 Model steel helmet and a side cap for summer use. The officer's kit was a knife and a pistol.

Date:	January 1943
Unit:	2nd Division, Finnish Army
Rank:	Captain
Theatre:	Eastern Front
Location:	around Leningrad

Lieutenant Finnish Army (Infantry) Karelia 1944

This lieutenant of the Finnish infantry is more notable for the aberrations of his uniform than for its typicality. The most visibly anachronistic item is the large and unwieldy helmet, the German 1915-pattern. By this point in the war, the 1915-pattern helmet had been replaced by the 1935-pattern of the regular German forces. His general appearance is closer to that of a World War I German infantryman than to a Finnish soldier. His short tunic and trousers are of poorer quality than the 1936-issue standard Finnish uniform, and they could be the pre-1936 reserve stock. Fortunately for him, he is well armed with a scarce Russian PPD-40G submachine gun. This most solid of weapons was more of a peacetime weapon, as it was manufactured to exceptionally high quality, higher quality than could be sustained during wartime production.

Date:	May 1944
Unit:	Infantry Division
Rank:	Lieutenant
Theatre:	Eastern Front
Location:	Karelia

Officer
French Cuirassier
France 1914

During the first year of World War I, many French units – particularly the cavalry units of cuirassiers, dragoons, hussars and chasseurs – wore service versions of full ceremonial dress that were highly decorative and coloured. However, by 1915 such units realized the hideous cost of high visibility, and modified their dress to be more in line with the infantry. Here we see a cuirassier officer decked out in this early ceremonial dress. The basic uniform is a dark-blue tunic with silver-threaded shoulder boards, over which is worn a gold-coloured gilet with red trim. Red cavalry breeches are worn with a pair of black riding boots. The striking shako hat, complete with horse-hair tail down the back, was often, as in this case, covered with a khaki cloth to avoid reflection off the bright metal badges, a draw for enemy snipers. This officer's regimental number is seen on his collar.

Date:	1914
Unit:	Cuirassier Cavalry Regiment
Rank:	Officer
Theatre:	Western Front
Location:	France

Private 1st Class French Army France 1914

This infantry soldier during the first year of World War I illustrates items of uniform which were wholly inappropriate to the conditions of combat on the Western Front. Chief amongst these is the red collar patches (the number indicating battalion or regiment), the red rank markings on the sleeve (a single chevron indicated Private 1st Class) and, the worst offenders, the bright-red trousers. The lessons of the low visibility, however, were quickly understood, and from September 1914 most French infantrymen arrived at the front line with blue linen overalls covering these scarlet trousers. The clean appearance of this soldier indicated that he has yet to reach the combat zone. He is wearing the French-issue leather webbing with M1897 ammunition pouches and, on his back, an M1893 pack with shelter-half strapped on top of it. The rifle he has been issued with is the 8mm (0.315in) Lebel M1886/93.

Date:	1914
Unit:	French Army
Rank:	Private 1st Class
Theatre:	Western Front
Location:	France

Corporal French Army Fort Vaux 1916

The Battle of Verdun was one of pure attrition, the strategy of General Erich von Falkenhayn to concentrate French forces in one position and there bleed France's military white. It did not succeed, but it cost the French 400,000 casualties, though the Germans lost 350,000. Fort Vaux was one of the fortifications at Verdun, and in this picture here we see an infantryman in the typical French uniform of the time; the horizon-blue uniform was introduced into the French forces in 1915, replacing a grey-green earlier version. The long grey-blue greatcoat features the rank of corporal on the sleeve. It was also in 1915 that the M1915 steel helmet was standardized, designed by August-Louis Adrian. The tunic underneath the greatcoat would have the regiment, battalion and arm-of-service identified on collar patches. This soldier has leather webbing and carries an 8mm (0.315in) 1892 revolver and an F1 hand-grenade.

Date:	1916
Unit:	French Army
Rank:	Corporal
Theatre:	Western Front
Location:	Fort Vaux

Lieutenant Escadrille N. No.3 Groupe de Chasse No.12, France 1916

Here we see Lieutenant Deullin, a distinguished French pilot of World War I, in the uniform of the French Aviation Militaire. The tunic is horizon-blue in colour with a stand-and-fall collar. On this collar is the insignia of a qualified aviator – a five-pointed winged star – while on his left breast is the stork badge of the Groupe de Chasse No.12 above two decoration ribbons. Rank is given on the dark-blue kepi hat and also on the sleeve of the tunic. The Aviation Militaire badge sits on the right breast. The tunic is worn with a pair of dark-blue breeches and a long pair of lace-up leather boots, which were worn by French aviators. Flying clothing consisted of a black leather jacket and trousers of a type actually used by the Paris Fire Brigade. A blue cloth armlet was used when wearing this dress to display the rank and group insignia.

Date:	1916
Unit:	No.3, Groupe de Chasse No.12
Rank:	Lieutenant
Theatre:	Western Front
Location:	France

Sergeant French Infantry France 1916

This soldier is wearing the standard horizon-blue uniform adopted in 1915, in addition to the helmet issued in the same year which was based upon a design from the French fire service. The collar number indicates either his regimental or battalion number, and rank is given conventionally on the sleeve of the greatcoat. Perhaps more interesting than the uniform is the weapon, the 8mm (0.315in) Chauchat M1915. Authorities have described the Chauchat as 'the worst machine gun in history'. The accusation is justified. The bolt travel in the gun was overlong and vigorous, disturbing accuracy, wearing out the parts, and pulling in dirt. It was made from poor-quality metals, frequently jammed, was awkward to load and let down the French infantry in combat. It is unclear how many French soldiers lost their lives because of its failures, but it was almost universally hated.

Date:	1917
Unit:	French Infantry
Rank:	Sergeant
Theatre:	Western Front
Location:	France

Private French Foreign Legion, Syria 1925

The French Foreign Legion were deployed to Syria in 1925 to combat the anti-French Djedel Druze rebel movement which was beginning to have serious military successes against French forces (Syria was placed under a French mandate just after the conclusion of World War I). In four months of campaigning, the Legion inflicted a series of crushing defeats upon the rebels, and further consolidated their reputation as masters of desert combat. Dress in the desert was rigorously practical. Here a private wears a loose cotton tunic and trousers, plus the traditional kepi – the white colour of these items would reflect away some of the sun's intense heat and glare. Footwear is a pair of brown shoes worn with long puttees to the knee to stop the intrusion of sand and wildlife. He is armed with the Artillery Musketoon Mle 1892, a carbine designed by André Berthier which had a five-round internal magazine.

Date:	1925
Unit:	French Foreign Legion
Rank:	Private
Location :	Syria
Conflict:	Syrian uprising

Major 46th Infantry Regiment Europe 1940

This French major's uniform, seen before France's surrender, harks back to the days of World War I in its style and colouring. Indeed, the major's participation in that conflict is made clear through the medal ribbons on his chest for the *Croix de Guerre* 1914–1918 in red and green, while the white and green ribbons relate to the bloody Dardanelles campaign. His unit number is stated on the collar tabs, though the khaki background of these patches and their dark-blue piping are also indicators of the 46th Infantry Regiment. A further unit identifier is the metal badge over the right breast pocket, and most infantry units would have their own versions of this. This officer displays his rank mainly on the sleeves of the tunic, though if he were wearing an overcoat the rank would be on a cloth panel attached to one of the coat buttons.

Date:	May 1940
Unit:	46th Infantry Regiment
Rank:	Major
Theatre:	North-west Europe
Location:	Edan

Sergeant Armoured Division Amiens 1940

This French Sergeant is wearing the typical uniform for an NCO of motorized troops in the early part of the war. The most distinctive item is the three-quarter length brown leather jacket issued from 1935. Here the rank of the sergeant is displayed by the single bar on the fastening seam of the coat, while the green patches (usually grey on most uniforms) on the collar indicate his unit. For headgear, the sergeant is wearing a blue beret featuring the badge of the French tank forces, representing crossed cannon and a medieval helmet. Underneath his left arm he carries the M35 padded helmet for wear inside the tank itself. This helmet, which was purpose-designed for mechanized warfare, was introduced in 1935. Prior to this time, the crewman would wear the standard infantry metal helmet, which turned out to be far from ideal in the cramped interior of a French tank in battle.

Date:	April 1940
Unit:	Armoured Division
Rank:	Sergeant
Theatre:	North-west Europe
Location:	Amiens

Private First Class 182nd Artillery Regiment Flanders 1940

The years 1935 and 1936 seem pivotal for uniform design in many European armies. Styles changed as the old ways of World War I were finally left behind. In the French Army prior to 1935, the uniform was the blue World War I pattern, but 1935 saw a khaki uniform, in line with many other nations, as shown here for this artillery private. This cut is perhaps superior, as he is wearing walking-out dress. The khaki tunic was single-breasted with six metal buttons and a low-fall collar, and had a gaberdine summer variant. Breeches were generally replaced by knickerbockers in 1938 for non-mounted soldiers. For headgear there was a blue or khaki kepi (seen here), a khaki field cap, and a steel helmet. Regimental number was usually on the kepi and the collar patches. This private has an artillery badge on his left sleeve, and his rank at the cuff.

Date:	April 1940
Unit:	182nd Artillery Regiment
Rank:	Private First Class
Theatre:	North-west Europe
Location:	Flanders

Private
Free French Army
England 1940

The Free French stationed in the UK, like many European soldiers who came to Britain following the German conquests in Europe, set their appearance somewhere between the British Army and their national force, now in exile. This private soldier is wearing the British khaki drill uniform. The tunic features a nationality title on the shoulder, while the red, white and blue ribbon on the shoulder-strap is a mark of allegiance to General de Gaulle, leader of the Free French Forces. However, there is still much more to emphasize his status as a French soldier. Most apparent is the French infantry helmet, the style having its origins back in 1915. By 1940 it was made of manganese steel, and was pressed as a single piece to improve its overall strength. An arm-of-service badge was fixed to the front. The boots, gas-mask case and load-carrying system is also French. His rifle, the Berthier M07/15, is the standard issue French rifle.

Date:	September 1940
Unit:	Free French Army
Rank:	Private
Theatre:	North-west Europe
Location:	England

Pilot
Paris Air Region
French Air Force
France 1940

Because of poor decisions in the armed forces in the interwar years, the French Air Force entered the war with many obsolescent aircraft. Indeed in May 1940, less than half of its 2200 aircraft were of modern specifications. This pilot of a Potez 63/II would have to fly hard to survive the might of the Luftwaffe. The standard uniform of French Air Force personnel was a dark Louise-Blue tunic and trousers and either a peaked cap (blue with a black band and gold-embroidered wings), a black beret (for working duties), or a steel helmet. A double-breasted greatcoat was also issued with a fall collar, a half-belt at the back, with gold-embroidered passants on the shoulders. The uniform in this case is covered by a one-piece flying overall, and the pilot wears a padded flying helmet of chrome leather. He carries the Chanole parachute.

Date:	April 1940
Unit:	Paris Air Region
Rank:	Pilot
Theatre:	North-west Europe
Location:	France

Lieutenant
Mediterranean Fleet
French Navy
Toulon 1940

Over 27 per cent of the French military budget was spent in the five years before the war on modernizing the navy. The consequence was that France entered the war with 660,000 tons of military shipping, the fourth largest fleet in the world, and possibly the most professional of the French arms-of-service. The sailor here is a lieutenant of the Mediterranean Fleet, and he wears the blue service dress of the navy, though in tropical climates there was also a standard lightweight khaki uniform. His cap is blue with a black leather peak, and features a badge depicting a gold-embroidered open laurel wreath with a fouled anchor at the centre. In addition to the blue service dress, officers had further options for dress uniform: the cap could feature a white cover with matching white trousers and shoes or even a white summer jacket.

Date:	May 1940
Unit:	Mediterranean Fleet
Rank:	Lieutenant
Theatre:	Mediterranean
Location:	Toulon

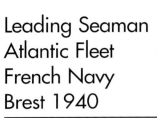

Leading Seaman Atlantic Fleet French Navy Brest 1940

Presenting arms with his 8mm (0.315in) M92/16 rifle and M92 knife bayonet, this French sailor is wearing the French Navy parade uniform. Some items of his uniform would only make an appearance in this context, such as the white laced and buckled gaiters which cover the tops of his boots. Others are part of the traditions of naval dress, some of them world-wide rather than purely French. The blue-and-white T-shirt, for example, is worn by several navies and navy-related special forces to this day. Though ceremonial in nature, this uniform also contains much of the standard dress. The tunic and trousers are general naval issue, the tunic having crossed anchors on the upper sleeve, while at the cuff are three stripes to indicate a junior quartermaster. The 'square rig' headgear, with the words 'Maritime Nationale', has a red pom-pom.

Date:	May 1940
Unit:	Atlantic Fleet
Rank:	Leading Seaman
Theatre:	Atlantic
Location:	Brest

Private
Vichy French
Moroccan Spahis
Syria 1941

The Vichy French forces of North Africa relied heavily on indigenous peoples to fill their ranks. In Syria in 1941 there was a total of 13 battalions plus one cavalry formation of African troops under the leadership of General Dentz. Moroccan, Algerian, Senegalese and Tunisian troops fought hard against the Allies for the Vichy cause, losing over 6000 men in Syria. Few ever went back to the Free French. This Moroccan soldier is wearing typical French uniform for the desert theatre (though a little heavily dressed compared to European troops) with a standard French helmet, khaki uniform, a long djellabah, and leather ammunition pouches. A yellow rank strip is buttoned to the front of his tunic, indicating *soldat de première classe*, while his helmet features a crescent to show his Muslim faith. Collar patches depict the regimental number.

Date:	July 1941
Unit:	Vichy French Moroccan Spahis
Rank:	Private
Theatre:	Mediterranean
Location:	Syria

Private French Volunteer Legion Ukraine 1943

This small contingent of French troops who fought on the Eastern Front for the Germans is a little-known aspect of French wartime history. The *Légion Volontaire Française* was an all-volunteer force which rose to 2452 men, motivated by everything from Nazi to anti-communist sympathies. This soldier is seen in the Ukraine, to which the volunteers were sent in June 1943, just over a year before they were disbanded in September 1944. German uniforms were adopted – the German greatcoat, 1935-pattern steel helmet, Mauser Kar 98k rifle and jackboots are standard German elements – yet the French tricolour adorn both the coat sleeve and the helmet, while the medals are French (left to right: Military Medal, Combatant's Cross, Colonial Medal with two bars). The rifle is also held high, in the style of the French.

Date:	June 1943
Unit:	French Volunteer Legion
Rank:	Private
Theatre:	Eastern Front
Location:	Ukraine

Goumier French African Troops Syria 1944

Large numbers of French African troops were recruited to the Allied cause with the fall of German forces in North Africa and the German occupation of Vichy France. These were formed into part of the French Expeditionary Corps which entered combat in Italy in 1943. As the war progressed, British and US uniforms dominated within the Free French, though many troops clung to their national identity. This Moroccan goumier is no exception. His vivid overcoat is the *djellabah*, an item of clothing which identified his tribe, and he wears a British steel helmet on top of his turban. The actual combat uniform, which can just be seen, is of US pattern, as is the webbing system: the pouches at the front would take clips for the M1 Garand rifle (though it is not clear here what rifle he is carrying, possibly a French-issue Lebel or Berthier).

Date:	May 1944
Unit:	French African troops
Rank:	Goumier
Theatre:	Mediterranean
Location:	Italy

Captain
Foreign Legion
Parachute Brigade
Indochina 1952

The war in Indochina between 1945 and 1954 was perhaps the bloodiest episode in all French Foreign Legion history, with 11,620 legionnaires killed out of the 20,000 who served there. For the 1 REP – the unit to which this Captain belongs – the six years between its formation in 1948 and the end of the war saw almost every single serving soldier either killed or wounded. French Foreign Legion uniform and kit in the first decade after the war is of mixed sources, testimony to their broad activities during World War II. This para captain in a camouflage US jungle-warfare jacket matched with the trousers of British airborne forces. The M1 helmet is American, as are the M1910 canteen cover and enamel water bottle, the ammunition pouch for pistol magazines, and the folding-stock M1A1 carbine. The backpack is British 1958-pattern.

Date:	1952
Unit:	1 REP
Rank:	Captain
Location:	Indochina
Conflict:	Indochina War 1945–54

Corporal French Colonial Parachute Regiment Suez Invasion 1956

Though the Anglo-French operation to seize the Suez Canal in 1956 was a generally calamitous mission, the French parachute forces performed excellently, partly owing to the thorough training and regimental pride, and partly to the fact that many of the paras were tough Indochina veterans. The soldier here shows the typical para uniform of the mid-1950s. The camouflage shirt and trousers are from the M51 parachute uniform (first issued in 1953) which, as the patterning suggests, was first intended for use by the paras in the jungles of South-east Asia. He also wears a pair of brown leather parachute high-boots and French webbing, and went into action at Suez heavily armed. His rifle, the 7.5mm (0.295in) MAS 1936 bolt-action, was boosted by six rifle-grenades fitted into a pouch system on his belt.

Date:	1956
Unit:	French Colonial Parachute Regiment
Rank:	Corporal
Location:	Port Fouad
Conflict:	Suez Invasion

Private French 10th Parachute Division Algeria 1961

The Algerian Independence War demonstrated how effective, and brutal, the French paras could be within a civil war/revolutionary conflict. Between 1957, when the 10th Parachute Division and 3rd Colonial Parachute Regiment were deployed, and July 1962, when Algeria achieved its independence, the paras perfected a style of counter-insurgency warfare which inflicted terrible losses on the nationalist ALN movement. Ultimately, it was their use of torture and murder that was their undoing, as the French military became vilified by the international press. This private is carrying a 7.5mm (0.295in) M1952 (AAT Mle 52) machine gun, a good attrition weapon for sudden encounters, and he is wearing the standard M51 tropical parachute uniform. By this time, all French troops were wearing camouflage, a change which occurred in 1960.

Date:	1961
Unit:	10th Parachute Division
Rank:	Private
Location:	Near Tunisian border
Conflict:	Algerian Independence War

Corporal French Foreign Legion Corsica 1990s

Except in parade dress, the French Foreign Legion have generally followed fairly spartan styles of uniform. What is constant is the infamous kepi hat. Two common types of service kepi prevail. This NCO gets to wear the *kepi noir*, a black-covered hat, while all lower ranks usually wear the *kepi blanc*, which has a white cover. The red top and gold badge are seen on both styles. This soldier is kitted out in standard khaki fatigues. The tunic features several regimental features and insignia. Running under the left arm is a regimental lanyard, next to various service medals. On the right breath is affixed the parachute brevet, which is seen on the uniforms of almost all personnel in the Legion, as almost everyone receives parachute training. Rank stripes are on the upper right sleeve. His weapon is the standard 5.56mm (0.22in) FAMAS F1 rifle.

Date:	1990s
Unit:	French Foreign Legion
Rank:	Corporal
Location:	Corsica
Conflict:	None

Operative French GIGN France 1990s

The *Groupe d'Intervention Gendarmeria Nationale* (GIGN) is France's foremost counter-terrorist unit, formed in 1974 as part of a general world-wide movement to establish effective national anti-terrorist squads. It has executed several dramatic and high-profile operations, including the liberation of Air France Flight 8969 from hijackers at Marseilles on 26 December 1994, which resulted in all terrorists killed for remarkably few hostage losses and injuries. This man is a GIGN sniper, indicated by his 7.62mm (0.3in) Giat FR-F2 precision weapon fitted with powerful optical sight. He wears thermal-imaging goggles for night-vision, featuring a built-in radio mike. Hanging from his belt is a fast-rope and harness, ideal for rapid deployment to a vantage point in an urban setting. The only markings on his uniform are a GIGN badge on his sleeve and parachute wings on his chest. All GIGN are parachute trained.

Date:	1990s
Unit:	GIGN
Rank:	Operative
Location:	France
Conflict:	None

Corporal Schutztruppe German East Africa 1914

The *Schutztruppe*, a small defence unit maintained by Germany in its East African colony, consisted of only 260 Germans and 2472 *askaris* (local soldiers), yet its training standards and tactical familiarity with the East African terrain enabled it to beat off a much larger British invasion force in November 1914. This corporal shows off typical *Schutztruppen* dress, distinct from that of German forces in northern Europe. The lightweight tunic and trousers are yellow khaki, the tunic featuring four patch pockets and a rounded fall collar. Rank is displayed on the sleeve while the epaulettes (white with a black-and-red twist) give unit identification. This soldier wears a slouch hat with the East African cockade on the side; the *askari* soldiers wore fez-like head-dress. The belt and pouches are standard German issue and the rifle is the 7.92mm (0.3in) Model M1891.

Date:	1914
Unit:	*Schutztruppe*
Rank:	Corporal
Theatre:	Africa
Location:	East Africa

Lieutenant-Captain Zeppelin Balloon Germany 1914

Zeppelin air-raids over England had little tactical significance in World War I, though the psychological effect was pronounced. Here we see *Kapitänleutnant* Joachim Breithaupt, commander of *L15*, dressed in usual clothing for the chilly operations over the south coast of England. Altitudes were very low by today's standards – up to 4877m (16,000ft) – yet in the unheated cockpit, this meant icy temperatures. To combat this, Breithaupt wears a base layer of a thick woollen jumper, over which he wears a naval double-breasted jacket featuring a German cross and rank markings on the cuffs, this being worn with leather trousers and a naval cap (this has the Imperial cockade surrounded by oak leaves and topped with a crown). The largest of Germany's Zeppelins – the *LZ-70* – was 220m (740ft) long with a range of 25,744km (16,000 miles), but after it was shot down, Germany ceased to use dirigibles for combat purposes.

Date:	1915
Unit:	Zeppelin
Rank:	Lieutenant-Captain
Theatre:	Western Front
Location:	Germany

Officer Uhlan (Lancer) Regiment Belgium 1915

The uhlans were one of several German cavalry divisions in World War I, the others including the cuirassiers, dragoons, hussars and *Jäger zu Pferde* (mounted rifles). Though the M1910 uniform – the standard uniform of German cavalry soldiers – worn by the uhlan officer here follows the general field-grey colour scheme which the regular army had adopted, the style is much more theatrical. Two features in particular capture the eye. The first, and most dominant, is the distinctive czapka helmet, here with a cockade on its plate. The khaki colour of the czapka is by virtue of a cover; in non-wartime scenarios the hat would be in the regimental colours. The other prominent item is the double-breasted tunic, featuring a stand-and-fall colour and displaying the arm-of-service in the trim and at the cuffs. This officer is armed with a Mauser C/96 pistol.

Date:	1915
Unit:	Uhlan Cavalry
Rank:	Officer
Theatre:	Western Front
Location:	Belgium

Lieutenant-Captain German Navy Jutland 1916

The uniform here was established within the German Navy in the early part of the twentieth century, though a full-length dress coat became popularly replaced by the double-breast tunic seen here. The typical dress of a German naval officer in the Great War was the blue tunic with matching trousers, a white shirt with wing collar and black tie, black shoes, and the naval peaked cap. The cap was blue in colour and had a black mohair surround and leather brim. It also featured Imperial cockade surrounded by oak leaves and surmounted by a crown. The rank of this officer is indicated by the rings on the sleeve capped by the Imperial crown, though naval officers during this period often had rank displayed through shoulder-boards and shoulder-straps. During the massive battle of Jutland, Germany's naval losses were less than Britain's, but it was no longer able to operate beyond the safety of the home ports.

Date:	1916
Unit:	German Navy
Rank:	Lieutenant-Captain
Theatre:	North Sea
Location:	Jutland

Private Württemberg Mountain Rifles Caporetto 1917

At the outset of World War I, most German infantry were clothed in field-grey uniforms. However, certain specialist units such as the *Jäger* and *Schützen* (Rifles) were issued grey-green uniforms, and into this category falls this soldier of the Württemberger Mountain Battalion, here pictured during the battle of Caporetto in 1917. The uniform consisted of a tunic with stand-and-fall collar, two patch pockets on the chest, and two slash side pockets covered with buttoned flaps. This was worn with a pair of matching trousers, high puttees and hobnailed boots. Headgear is a simple grey-green Bergmütze field cap. The Württemberg unit is indicated by the collar patches (the single pip on these shows the rank), the piping around the shoulder and the lanyard on the left hip. He is wearing standard German infantry equipment and carries a 7.92mm (0.3in) M98 carbine.

Date:	1917
Unit:	Württemberg Mountain Rifles
Rank:	Private
Theatre:	Italian Front
Location:	Caporetto

Stormtrooper Michael Offensive Western Front 1918

The stormtroopers were a new breed of soldier trained and developed by Germany between 1914 and 1915. The concept, devised mainly by *Hauptmann* Erich Rohr, was for spearhead units, *Sturmtruppen*, to use speed, mobility and firepower to smash open weak points in enemy defences for mass infantry assault to widen. In December 1915 an operational unit, the *Sturm-Bataillon Rohr*, entered into the war. Here we see a soldier during the Michael Offensive, Germany's last-ditch effort to break the deadlock of the Western Front in 1918. His medieval appearance was typical of assault troops. Metal body armour, a chain-mail head-dress and non-standard steel helmet gave protection in trench battles, though at the expense of mobility. This soldier is armed with classic trench fighting tools: a Mauser Model 1914 pistol and two hand-grenades, as well as a sharpened spade.

Date:	1918
Unit:	*Sturmtruppen* Assault Units
Rank:	Trooper
Theatre:	Western Front
Location:	Between Flesquières and St Quentin, France

Stormtrooper German Army France 1918

This stormtrooper carries little extraneous kit. The two khaki bags slung over his shoulders are actually grenade sacks made from sandbags, a plentiful supply of grenades being requisite for most stormtroopers assaulting Allied trenches. In addition he carries a gas mask case, a long-handled shovel and a 7.9mm (0.31in) Mauser carbine. The M1915 uniform is typical of the German soldier in 1918. It replaced the M1910 as the standard-issue German army blouse in 1915 and initially featured exposed buttons. These were eventually covered with a fly front, as shown here, something which gave less for enemy riflemen to draw a bead on. Note how this soldier has camouflaged his helmet. This was only done by German stormtroopers and was the first effective use of infantry camouflage. Each man would paint an individual pattern, but based around an angular disruptive-type design scheme.

Date:	1918
Unit:	German Army
Rank:	Stormtrooper
Theatre:	Western Front
Location:	France

Pilot
Condor Legion
Madrid 1939

The Condor Legion was a force of some 100 German aircraft (split equally between bombers and fighters) and over 16,000 personnel which fought for the Nationalist cause in the Spanish Civil War. Hitler deployed the force in November 1936, and the conflict gave German aviators and many ground troops – the Legion also featured anti-tank, anti-aircraft and armoured units – opportunities for combat experience prior to World War II. Perhaps the most significant aerial tactics to emerge were the deployment of fighters in the four-aircraft *Schwarme* and also dive-bombing. The pilot here, pictured late in the campaign, is wearing a German aviator's cap, jacket and pantaloons, all in a dark khaki. On the right breast pocket hangs a 'Spanish Cross' German campaign medal, above which is the brevet of the Spanish air force. His boots are those of an officer, these being made of leather and suede and lined with lambswool.

Date:	May 1939
Unit:	Condor Legion
Rank:	Pilot
Location:	Madrid
Conflict:	Spanish Civil War

Corporal Infantry Regiment Poland 1939

A German corporal strides forward during the first few victorious months of *Blitzkrieg* in the West. Because of Germany's intensive pre-war investment in its armed forces, German soldiers at this stage of the war tend to be seen with an excellent standard of uniform and kit (compare this image with those of German soldiers on the Eastern Front in 1945). The blouse is in infantry field-grey, featuring a dark-blue collar on which the artificial silk-thread rank stripes are stitched; other rank markings are on the shoulder-straps. Trousers come in a slightly darker stone-grey. Other insignia is fairly minimal, mainly Nazi or national emblems on the blouse breast or the helmet. His weapon – the MP38 submachine gun, indicated by the long magazine pouches worn over the stomach – shows that he is a section leader in charge of a squad of 10 soldiers.

Date:	September 1939
Unit:	Infantry Regiment
Rank:	Corporal
Theatre:	Eastern Europe
Location:	Poland

Seaman
German Navy
Baltic 1939

This seaman, who is operating in the Baltic, is wearing the standard summer whites of the German Navy in the months immediately prior to the onset of war. The fact that hostilities have not been declared is indicated by the name of the ship still being displayed on the cap band; names were omitted on wartime caps for security reasons. Furthermore, the white cap-cover worn here was not used once war had begun. The cap features a Nazi eagle set above a national cockade – a standard insignia for ratings – while on the tunic, the national emblem is stitched over the right breast. Officers who were wearing the summer uniform would generally have a metallic pin badge depicting the eagle. By 1943 the standard summer dress would have changed to include a light-brown uniform with a peaked field cap, and this particular style was one which had some resemblance to the dress of the Africa Corps.

Date:	September 1939
Unit:	German Navy
Rank:	Seaman
Theatre:	Germany
Location:	Baltic Sea

Corporal
1st Panzer Regiment
France 1940

German uniform designers in the mid-1930s managed to create uniforms which were both functional and visually impressive, and nowhere is this more apparent than in the case of this corporal from the 1st Panzer Regiment. The uniform – introduced into service in 1935 – is an ideal form of dress for the cramped and hot interior of an armoured vehicle. The trousers are loose to aid movement and ventilation, and the double-breasted jacket is kept short so that buttons are not strained in a seated position. The beret appears soft, but actually contains extensive padding for head protection. Insignia relating to arm-of-service features on the collar patches – skull-and-crossbones on a black background – while this soldier also has the Iron Cross and Tank Battle Badge on the left breast. A pistol would usually be the only weapon carried for self defence and most personal items would be stored in the vehicle.

Date:	May 1940
Unit:	1st Panzer Regiment
Rank:	Corporal
Theatre:	Western Europe
Location:	France

Major Heinkel He111 Luftflotte 2 France 1940

With the approach of summer during the Battle of Britain campaign, many German airmen began to wear the one-piece canvas flying suit designed for summer use. Its canvas construction made it lighter and more breathable, and the pockets were set inside the overalls to avoid bulky padded sections. Headgear in this case is the Luftwaffe peaked cap rather than the beige linen flight helmet usually worn on operations. This cap features the Luftwaffe eagle, cockade, oak leaves and wings, while the chin-strap is in the silver of officer rank. The actual rank of major is depicted by the two bars and propeller badge on the sleeve. A yellow life-jacket is worn against the very real possibility of ditching in the North Sea or English Channel. Many German aircraft succumbed to fuel shortages on the way home and were forced into the sea.

Date:	July 1940
Unit:	Luftflotte 2
Rank:	Major
Theatre:	North-west Europe
Location:	France

NCO
1st Parachute Regiment
Belgium 1940

The German Airborne forces invested heavily is designing a practical and functional parachute uniform, though the RZ1 and RZ16 parachutes gave the para no directional control of flight and hung the para in the straps at an oblique angle. This para wears a jump-smock typical of the summer of 1940, though field-grey seems more common than khaki. The smock, worn over the regular uniform, was removed by zip on landing (although the parachute harness had no quick-release mechanism). By 1941 a second pattern smock came in a Splitter (splinter) camouflage. The helmet is a para type designed not to snag on ropes, while kapok-filled kneepads protect the legs. Para boots featured thick, rubber soles to prevent slipping inside an aircraft.

Date:	August 1940
Unit:	1st Parachute Regiment
Rank:	NCO
Theatre:	North-west Europe
Location:	Belgium

Lieutenant Jagdgeschwader 26, III Gruppe Pas de Calais 1940

Pictured here is Luftwaffe fighter pilot *Leutnant* Joachim Müncheburg, a highly decorated airman of JG26 who shot down 135 Allied aircraft before being killed in action in 1943. The decorations on display are the Iron Cross 1st and 2nd Class, and the Knight's Cross, sitting alongside pilot and wound badges. The blue-grey uniform was Luftwaffe standard, its heritage dating back to the dress adopted by the German Air Sport Association in 1933. The tunic was single-breasted with two chest patch pockets and two side patch pockets, and rank displayed in white on gold collar patches and on the shoulder-straps. The trousers were breeches, as seen here, or straight leg, worn with high boots or black shoes respectively. Finishing the dress was the peaked cap, which had an artificial mohair band, silver cords and Luftwaffe insignia.

Date:	September 1940
Unit:	Jagdgeschwader 26
Rank:	Lieutenant
Theatre:	North-west Europe
Location:	Pas de Calais

Lance-Corporal Panzer Lehr Regiment Eastern Front 1941

This soldier – Lance-Corporal Freidhelm Ollenschäger – is wearing the standard uniform of an armoured crewman: black loose trousers and short double-breasted jacket. Instead of the padded beret, he has a cloth side cap. His rank is displayed as a single stripe on the sleeve and the Wehrmacht eagle and the death's-head badge on the collar patches indicate his arm-of-service. The standard 45mm (1.8in) wide German Army belt would have been worn by all German Army soldiers up to officer rank, and even in many situations beyond. It served for all circumstances, both operational and parade, coming in black or dark brown, though occasionally lighter brown versions are seen. The highly visible aluminium belt buckle (Koppelschloss), painted field-grey, often bore the legend *Gott Mit Uns* ('God With Us').

Date:	July 1941
Unit:	Panzer Lehr Regiment
Rank:	Lance-Corporal
Theatre:	Eastern Front
Location:	Western USSR

Corporal
15th Panzer Division
North Africa 1941

Naturally, when the armoured units of the German Army transferred to the North African theatre, the black uniform of European zones was no longer appropriate. Thus we tend to see armoured crews adopting the standard khaki uniform of the Africa Corps, as seen here consisting of a khaki tunic with lighter open-neck shirt beneath, and breeches or straight trousers. Footwear is a pair of leather and suede knee-high lace-up boots, which tended to be rejected for shorter, cooler boots in the arid desert conditions. Indeed, flexibility and customization were the watchwords of desert dress. The baking temperatures meant that uniform codes were little enforced as each soldier adapted as best he could to the heat. This soldier wears army uniform, but retains the death's-head collar insignia of the armoured forces, as a simple badge.

Date:	July 1941
Unit:	15th Panzer Division
Rank:	Corporal
Theatre:	Mediterranean
Location:	North Africa

Captain Luftwaffe, Army Group Centre Ukraine 1942

Captain Hans Phillipp, pictured here, was one of Germany's most highly decorated pilots on the Eastern Front. He was awarded the Swords to the Knight's Cross of the Iron Cross with Oak Leaves for downing 82 Allied aircraft, and he would go on to take many more. However, such victories in Russia were offset by the chronic problems of supply and maintenance which had beset the Luftwaffe by the end of 1941, as well as improvements in Soviet fighter aircraft and tactics. Captain Phillipp's decoration is displayed by the cross around his neck, while the yellow collar patches show the oak leaves and acorns (the three silver wings on the same patches and the two yellow pips on the shoulder-straps indicate the rank). A flying badge is worn on the left breast, and the yellow colouration in the insignia refers to the arm-of-service.

Date:	March 1942
Unit:	Luftwaffe
Rank:	Captain
Theatre:	Eastern Front
Location:	Ukraine

Private 389th Infantry Division Stalingrad 1943

This soldier here stands as a salutary counterpoint to the crisp images of German uniform seen earlier in this section. This soldier has been drawn from a Soviet newsreel of captured German soldiers after the catastrophe of Stalingrad. Some 90,000 German soldiers went into captivity under the Russians. Only 5000 emerged alive, some up to 13 years after the war. The hideous deficiencies in German winter uniform are apparent here. He has wrapped a cloth around his head to protect himself from frostbite, and his greatcoat is stuffed with newspaper and straw. He has also managed to acquire a pair of straw overboots, usually issued to sentries or similar soldiers who would have to stand for long periods. The bag he carries in his left hand is the M1931 clothing bag which would have been used to store changes of clothes.

Date:	2 February 1943
Unit:	389th Infantry Division
Rank:	Private
Theatre:	Eastern Front
Location:	Stalingrad

Corporal *Hermann Göring* Panzer Division Mareth 1943

The Luftwaffe had several élite ground force units under its command during World War II, not least the unit which took its commander-in-chief's name, the *Hermann Göring* Panzer Division. This soldier is seen during the division's operations in North Africa in 1943 in the ultimately futile defence of Tunisia. He wears a khaki uniform which includes trousers with buckle ankles, hence the baggy appearance. His 'jacket' is actually a shelter quarter in the splinter camouflage used by the Luftwaffe ground forces. He is heavily armed with two *Stielgranate* (stick-grenades) and an MP38 or MP40, this weapon indicated by the long magazine pouches on the belt. Identification with the *Hermann Göring* Division came from a blue cuffband on the right cuff, featuring 'Hermann Göring' in white on a blue background.

Date:	March 1943
Unit:	Hermann Göring Panzer Division
Rank:	Corporal
Theatre:	Mediterranean
Location:	Mareth, Tunisia

107

Corporal
Das Reich Division
Kharkov 1943

The *Das Reich* Division was one of the SS's premier front-line units. This corporal's SS membership is stated through several items of insignia around his field-grey uniform. Working from the top, we have the death's-head badge dominating the peaked service-dress cap, while on the right collar of the tunic there is the double lightning flash runes of the SS. Note that the left collar was always reserved for rank, the other rank marking being on the shoulder-straps and also the two lace rings around the tunic cuffs. The German eagle on the left sleeve was another SS trait. The SS eagle went through two main forms in the SS, a small pointed-wing variety in the 1930s, followed by a larger eagle with a longer middle section of each wing and also larger in proportion to the wreath. This soldier is emphatically SS, an allegiance proclaimed in words on his belt buckle: *Mein Ehre heisst Treue* ('Loyalty is my Honour').

Date:	June 1943
Unit:	Das Reich Division
Rank:	Corporal
Theatre:	Eastern Front
Location:	Kharkov

Sergeant-Major 1st Airborne Division Italy 1943

The early years of World War II saw German paras with their own designated uniforms. Yet by 1943 – by which time airborne forces were suffering horrific losses on the Eastern Front – general issue equipment was becoming more commonplace, especially as post-Crete, the paras did not engage in any major parachute operations again. This soldier still has two items of para issue: the FG42 rifle, which was essentially one of the first modern assault rifles produced and was designed specifically for para usage, and the para helmet, with chicken wire added for fitting foliage for camouflage. The overcoat is the Luftwaffe field coat in splinter camouflage for use by ground personnel, here with matching triple pouches for ammunition. Luftwaffe tropical trousers are also worn with buckles at the ankles.

Date:	June 1943
Unit:	1st Airborne Division
Rank:	Sergeant-Major
Theatre:	Mediterranean
Location:	Italy

Sergeant
Grossdeutschland
Division
Kursk 1943

The *Grossdeutschland* Panzergrenadier Division, an élite, multi-arm force within the German Army, had infantry, artillery and armour in regimental- or battalion strengths. Pride within the unit ran strong, a pride it displayed in uniform insignia and combat badges. This uniform, that of a panzergrenadier, is in field-grey, as he belongs to an assault-gun detachment. Membership of the division was indicated by the letters 'GD' displayed on shoulder-straps, the border of which would denote the arm-of-service within the division (this soldier has the red border for artillery). The élite status of the *Grossdeutschland* is suggested here by the sergeant's Knight's Cross, the Iron Cross 1st and 2nd Class, the General Assault badge, and the wound badge. Two bands around his right arm show he has single-handedly destroyed two tanks.

Date:	July 1943
Unit:	*Grossdeutschland* Division
Rank:	Sergeant
Theatre:	Eastern Front
Location:	Kursk

Private
Leibstandarte
Division
Poland 1944

The *Leibstandarte* Adolf Hitler division was the first division of the SS. Like many Waffen-SS units, they performed some heroic actions during the Eastern Front campaigns, alongside the less-than-heroic crimes which often accompanied their political role. This tankman wears a 1944-issue camouflage two-piece in a distinctive foliage pattern. The SS were the pioneers of camouflage during World War II and, as far back as 1940, issued camouflage uniforms. The uniform here replaced a one-piece camouflage overall of 1941, after when the SS went through two subsequent patterns: the M43 with single-breasted jacket and the M44 with double-breasted shirt. Four types of camouflage were utilized, known as 'palm tree', 'pea', 'oak leaf' and 'plane tree' to indicate their natural patterns.

Date:	April 1944
Unit:	*Leibstandarte* Division
Rank:	Private
Theatre:	Eastern Front
Location:	Poland

Private *Hitlerjugend* Division Normandy 1944

By 1944, camouflage was making widespread appearance in many German units, though mainly those units with elite status. While much of this camouflage was confined to the Eastern Front initially, the threat of a second front in France forced Hitler to relocate some SS units there. This *Hitlerjugend* trooper is wearing an Italian pattern camouflage smock and trousers, the helmet also being covered in a matching cloth. The period 1944–45 saw many German units adopting surplus Italian military clothing, as Germany's own supplies ran short and industry could not produce enough to meet demand. This accounts for an increasing lack of consistent appearance amongst German troops on all fronts. The *Hitlerjugend* division was largely formed from former members of the Hitler Youth. This trooper is armed with the MG42 machine gun.

Date:	June 1944
Unit:	*Hitlerjugend* Division
Rank:	Private
Theatre:	North-west Europe
Location:	Normandy

Senior Sergeant 916th Infantry Regiment Normandy 1944

This image of a German *Feldwebel* (sergeant) shows the equipment carried by German infantry soldiers in 1944. The most recognizable item is the cylindrical gas mask case. This was made of fluted steel and featured a hinged lid containing additional eyepieces for the mask. Beneath this to right is the tent quarter/poncho known as the Zeltbahn 31, rendered in the distinctive Splitter (splinter) camouflage designed for army use in the 1930s. The Zeltbahn could be used as a wind shelter, a tent, a poncho, or even be made into an emergency stretcher. The two remaining items around the soldier's back are a canvas bread bag and a water bottle in leather cover. On the belt can be seen an ammunition pouch for his Mauser rifle. The rest of the uniform is standard German issue for this stage of the war, while the helmet has a wire cover for attaching camouflage.

Date:	6 June 1944
Unit:	916th Infantry Regiment
Rank:	Senior Sergeant
Theatre:	North-west Europe
Location:	Normandy

Major
Stukageschwader
Russia 1944

The airman here is Major Hans-Ulrich Rudel, a talented German Stuka veteran who was awarded the Knight's Cross with Sword and Oak Leaves for bravery and performance (the award can be seen here at the collar). He was shot down no less than 32 times. He is wearing what was often termed the 'Invasion Suit', a one-piece flying overall in field-grey, with zip fastenings at the front and down the insides of the legs, the latter so that the outfit could be removed even while wearing boots or shoes. The large patch pockets served to store maps and navigational aids, and even basic survival equipment in case of being shot down. When wearing such an overall over the standard uniform, the rank and arm-of-service of NCOs and officers were displayed on the shoulder-straps and collar patches, and sometimes on the upper sleeve of a flying jacket. The shoulder-straps were double silver cords, interlaced for senior officers.

Date:	August 1944
Unit:	Stukageschwader 2
Rank:	Major
Theatre:	Eastern Front
Location:	Western USSR

Petty Officer
Kriegsmarine
Kiel 1944

The severe Baltic winter required that all members of the Kriegsmarine wear specialist clothing for their own protection. The petty officer here is in the foul-weather clothing issued to all seaman on either Baltic or Atlantic duties. In this case it consists of a thick padded coat over waterproof jacket and trousers, with sea boots and waterproof mittens. A traditional sou'wester hat is also worn. Rank is given on the collar patches (one stripe for a petty officer), introduced in blue in December 1939, and via the anchor on the sleeve of the coat which was also often worn with departmental badges. This would have protected the soldier while on the arduous convoy or minelaying duties which the German Navy conducted in the Baltic. An alternative to the short jacket was a heavy lined watchcoat which had reinforced shoulders. In 1943 a sand-coloured tropical uniform was introduced for the summer months.

Date:	August 1944
Unit:	Kriegsmarine
Rank:	Petty Officer
Theatre:	Baltic
Location:	Kiel

Auxiliary Flak Unit Leipzig 1944

The Baltic states yielded surprisingly fruitful recruiting grounds for the German forces following their occupation in 1941. This soldier is actually a Latvian national. A wave of Latvians were recruited into Luftwaffe formations from September 1943, ultimately forming the Latvian Aviation League in August 1944. However, other Latvians entered the Luftwaffe after being rejected for combat service with ground units, and many of these became auxiliaries in flak units. Appropriate to his apparent age, this soldier is wearing a field-grey Hitler Youth uniform. It is relatively unadorned, the principal insignia being the Latvian national emblem worn just above the cap band and also on the sleeve. Auxiliaries in flak units were known as *Flakhelfer*, though many were absorbed into the SS during the latter months of the war, and subsequently they were termed *SS-Zoglinge*.

Date:	September 1944
Unit:	Flak Unit
Rank:	Auxiliary
Theatre:	Germany
Location:	Leipzig

Private/Recruit 1st Airborne Division Germany 1985

A German *Fallschirmjäger* prepares to perform a static-line training jump during exercises in the mid-1980s. His uniform still follows the style of outfit worn by the paras in World War II, though with modern updates in material and utility. The para helmet remains in the high-side shape, allowing good hearing aboard a noisy aircraft and giving little for parachute lines to snag upon. He wears a two-piece jump uniform consisting of field-grey shirt and stone-grey trousers, with the colours of the German Federal Republic on his left tunic sleeve and few other insignia. This probably indicates a recruit status, also suggested by the fact that the soldier is jumping without any weaponry or pack. His goal is the red beret desired by many para recruits world-wide, though for Germans, the badge is that of a diving eagle, the *Fallschirmjäger*'s emblem.

Date:	1985
Unit:	1st Airborne Division
Rank:	Private/Recruit
Location:	Germany
Conflict:	None

Operative GSG-9 Anti-Terrorist Unit Germany 1990s

The *Grenzschutzgruppe-9* (GSG-9) ranks alongside the SAS Counter-Revolutionary Warfare team as one of the best hostage-rescue and anti-terrorist units in the world. Their formation was inspired by the débâcle at Munich in 1972, when a botched police rescue-attempt resulted in nine kidnapped Israeli athletes at the Munich Olympics being massacred by their captors. GSG-9 was established to create an efficient, standardized response force to national emergencies. Here we see an operative in classic urban-combat gear, with the suggestion of a helicopter deployment lying in his airborne harness for fast-roping down to buildings. His helmet is para-style, the high-side sections allowing good hearing, while a balaclava protects anonymity. His weapon, the 9mm HK MP5A3, is the choice of HRU teams world-wide for its stopping power.

Date:	1990s
Unit:	*Grenzschutzgruppe-9*
Rank:	Operative
Location:	Germany
Conflict:	None

Private Evzones Greek Army Greece 1940

Mussolini's invasion of Greece in 1941 was conducted under the belief that Italian forces would soon subdue an inferior Greek Army. However, Greek forces violently repelled the Italian onslaught through dextrous tactics, intimacy with the mountainous terrain, and sheer aggression, and German forces were deployed in rescue in April 1940. This soldier belongs to the *Evzones* infantry, an élite force within the Greek Army formed during the early 1800s in Greece's independence wars and absorbed into the Greek Army in 1833. This uniform shows elements of the *Evzones* traditional dress, including the shoes with woollen pom-poms. The tight pantaloons and stockings are a military representation of civilian mountain dress. For warmth, this soldier has a local goat-fleece cape.

Date:	February 1940
Unit:	*Evzones*
Rank:	Private
Theatre:	Balkans
Location:	Greece

Lieutenant Artillery Regiment Greek Army Greece 1940

As a mounted officer, this artillery lieutenant wears loose riding breeches and leather riding boots, these being worn with a three-quarter length tunic fastened at the waist with a Sam Browne belt. The uniform is matched by a khaki kepi hat, this being adorned with a silver crown and also the blue-and-white Greek cockade. Black stripes delineate the rank, as do the stars on the shoulder-straps (the collar patches indicate the arm-of-service), though the placing of rank on the kepi exists only on pre-war versions. Other headgear issued to officers included a khaki peaked cap as an alternative to the kepi, a side cap, and also a steel helmet which even officers would wear into combat. This helmet moved from British-pattern to a native Greek pattern during the first two years of the war. For equipment, this officer is carrying binoculars and a map case.

Date:	October 1940
Unit:	Artillery Regiment
Rank:	Lieutenant
Theatre:	Balkans
Location:	Greece

Wing Commander Fighter Squadron Greek Air Force Greece 1941

The Greek Air Force uniform was designed around the British Royal Air Force model, and many Greek pilots underwent their primary combat training in the UK. A single-breasted jacket and matching trousers, both in blue-grey, was the standard uniform and was worn with a white or grey shirt and black tie. The peaked cap featured a black leather peak, black mohair band, plus a gold-embroidered eagle on the front set in a crest and crown motif. This uniform would naturally vary considerably in operational settings; khaki drill uniforms, for instance, are often seen in the summer months of combat. Rank markings on this officer are found in the stripes and diamond on the cuffs which, combined with the row of gold-embroidered oak leaves on the cap peak, indicate a senior officer (junior officers would not wear this detail).

Date:	March 1941
Unit:	Fighter Squadron
Rank:	Wing Commander
Theatre:	Balkans
Location:	Greece

Able Seaman Greek Navy Greece 1941

Like the Greek Air Force to the Royal Air Force, the Greek Navy had a uniform similar to that of the Royal Navy. This able seaman wears the classic blue reefer jacket with matching trousers and Royal Navy-pattern anklets. As a rating, his rank is given on the sleeve in red (the chevron indicates the rank of able seaman, the torpedo beneath signifies a torpedo specialist), whereas officers would have their rank displayed via embroidery on the cuff and also on the shoulder-straps of the greatcoat or tunic. Though the uniform here is of a Royal Navy style, the equipment and firearm are all Greek Army issue. The rifle is the 6.5mm (0.255in) Carbine Model 1914, a shortened Greek version of the Mannlicher, with fittings for the long bayonet which extends down his left leg (earlier carbine models had no bayonet fittings). Two ammunition pouches fitted to the leather belt hold five-round chargers for the rifle's rotary magazine.

Date:	April 1941
Unit:	Greek Navy
Rank:	Able Seaman
Theatre:	Mediterranean
Location:	Greece

Private Greek National Army Greece 1947

During the post-war conflict between the nationalist government of Greece and communist revolutionaries, both the UK and the US sponsored government resistance with both men and materiel (the British were initially involved as a combat force, but economic austerity at home forced their withdrawal). In terms of uniform and kit, two periods of influence can be identified: 1945–1947, when British equipment and clothing dominates; and 1947, when US materiel increasingly takes over. The soldier shown here straddles these two periods. His shirt, pullover, beret, anklets and trousers are standard British Army uniform (the trousers are 'denims', a working version of combat uniform). By contrast, the submachine gun is the US .45in Thompson M1A1, which was widely known a powerful close-quarters weapon.

Date:	1947
Unit:	Greek National Army
Rank:	Private
Location:	Northern Greece
Conflict:	Greek Civil War

Guerrilla
Greek
Democratic Army
Greece 1947

The communist revolutionary forces of the *Dimokratikos Stratos Ellados* (DSE) conducted an effective guerrilla war against the Greek Government for nearly three years, yet eventually sabotaged its own efforts by moving too quickly to conventional warfare in 1948. After this point, the DSE insurgents were more easily targeted by the US-backed forces of the Greek National Army, and several set-piece battles saw the DSE take losses it could not sustain. This fighter is seen in 1947, wearing a civilian blouse and waistcoat, but with trousers from British Army combat dress, here dyed black. The web anklets are also British Army stock. She carries the 9mm MP40 submachine gun, no doubt left by the wartime German forces. The DSE had no standard weapons and uniform, though many DSE units shared khaki battledress and a khaki side cap.

Date:	1947
Unit:	Greek Democratic Army
Rank:	Guerrilla
Location:	Greece
Conflict:	Greek Civil War

Sergeant Hungarian Gendarmerie Russia 1941

As in the case of the German Army, the undoing of the Hungarian forces was its commitments on the Eastern Front. The 2nd Hungarian Army alone suffered up to 190,000 casualties during its ill-fated defence on the Soviet Don Front to the south of Voronezh, near Stalingrad, in 1943. However, this soldier is pictured in earlier times, part of the Hungarian Mobile Corps under General Ferenc Szombathelyi. He represents the élite Royal Hungarian Gendarmerie. The khaki tunic and trousers are standard Hungarian Army wear, the tunic featuring a stand-and-fall collar (with rank and arm-of-service displayed on patches), five buttons down the front and four pleated patch pockets, two front, two side. A most distinctive element of the uniform is the side cap featuring cockerel feather plume. The sergeant also wears a whistle on a green lanyard with pom-poms.

Date:	July 1941
Unit:	Hungarian Gendarmerie
Rank:	Sergeant
Theatre:	Eastern Front
Location:	Southern Russia

Infantryman Rifle Brigade 2nd Hungarian Army Russia 1942

Seen here in November 1942, this soldier of the 2nd Hungarian Army presents a defiant picture in his role as company bugler. The uniform is the Hungarian Army pattern introduced in 1922, though the helmet is recognizably of German origin; Hungarian forces wore both the 1915- and 1935-pattern of German helmet. Other headgear included a side cap and a peaked field cap. The tunic was a single-breasted khaki affair with two breast- and two side pockets and a stand-and-fall collar, while the unusual pantaloons featured buttons to create a tight fit around the calf and an integral anklet to fit over the tops of the boots. Over this uniform this soldier wears a greatcoat, and he carries a cow-hide pack on his back with a red-hair decoration which alludes to colours of Imperial Austria.

Date:	November 1942
Unit:	Rifle Brigade
Rank:	Infantryman
Theatre:	Eastern Front
Location:	Southern Russia

2nd Lieutenant 1st Armd. Division Hungarian Army Russia 1943

This 2nd Lieutenant wears the typical uniform of a tank crewman for the mid years of the war. It consists of a single-piece cotton khaki overall, over which he wears a leather waistcoat. The uniform is completed with a side cap which features a cockade badge in national colours. At the beginning of the war, a double-breasted leather jacket was the standard, this being worn with an Italian black-leather tank helmet which featured a neckflap. This was steadily replaced by the outfit seen here, as Hungary took more of a lead on uniform design from its German allies. Equipment here is minimal, as you would expect with tank crews. On his belt he carries a pistol in a holster, probably a Hungarian 9mm Pistol 39M. By 1943 the Hungarian 1st Armoured Division was decimated, tactically and materially outclassed by the Soviet T-34 formations.

Date:	January 1943
Unit:	1st Armoured Division
Rank:	2nd Lieutenant
Theatre:	Eastern Front
Location:	Southern Russia

Lieutenant Fighter Squadron Hungarian Air Force Russia 1943

Beneath his German sheepskin flying jacket, this lieutenant of the Hungarian Air Force is wearing standard Hungarian Army khaki service dress, including a khaki field cap with brown leather peak. The army uniform was worn by all pilot- and ground personnel, as the Hungarian Air Force actually belonged to the Army. Much of the distinction from the army is made in insignia. The cap has the usual Hungarian cockade in the centre-front, but features air-force wings on the left side. Rank here is displayed in patches on the jacket sleeves, a typical site for flying officers and NCOs. However, when wearing only the tunic, officer rank would be on the shoulder-straps, with all lower ranks having cuff patches. This lieutenant is dressed for the spring of southern Russia, but by winter he would wear a black, zip-fastened leather flying suit.

Date:	May 1943
Unit:	Fighter Squadron
Rank:	Lieutenant
Theatre:	Eastern Front
Location:	Southern Russia

Guerrilla Revolutionary Forces Budapest 1956

On 23 October 1956, what began as a peaceful student protest in Budapest against Communist government policies turned into a revolutionary action backed by the Hungarian armed forces. By 1 November, Hungarian Government officials announced the withdrawal of Hungary from the Warsaw Pact. The Soviet Union responded by a large deployment of armour in Budapest, forcibly returning Hungary to the fold, though only after bloody fighting. This revolutionary wears civilian hat, trousers and boots, but the rest of his dress and equipment is from Hungarian military stocks (the army opened up many of its depots for the revolutionaries). Over his khaki tunic he wears a Sam Browne belt from which hangs a pouch of Soviet grenades, and his rifle is a Soviet 7.62mm (0.3in) M1944 bolt-action carbine, which would have been outdated against the Russian Kalashnikov assault rifles.

Date:	1956
Unit:	Revolutionary Forces
Rank:	Guerrilla
Location:	Budapest
Conflict:	Hungarian Uprising

Sergeant
8th Indian Division
Indian Army
North Africa 1940

As soldiers of the British Empire, Indian Army troops used British Army-style uniforms and kit, though with many national variations. This soldier is wearing standard British Army drill kit issued during World War II: a khaki shirt and shorts, long woollen socks, and black shoes. Prior to the war, Indian Army forces wore a variety of khaki and silver-grey shirts, meaning a fluctuation in appearance throughout its ranks, though by 1942 standardization in favour of the British patterns was established. The webbing is the older 1908-pattern (the 1936-pattern became the standard for British Army troops during the war) but this sergeant also has a local chest pouch and leather ammunition pouch and pistol holster. He is carrying the precarious Molotov cocktails in his right hand and the No. 36 British hand-grenades in his left.

Date:	December 1940
Unit:	8th Indian Division
Rank:	Sergeant
Theatre:	Mediterranean
Location:	North Africa

Corporal
9th Gurkha Rifles
Indian Army
Malaya 1941

This soldier belongs to the 9th Gurkha Rifles of the 11th Indian Division, the Gurkhas having served with the British Army since the nineteenth century. The uniform resembles British Army tropical dress, though with some variations. Most apparent of these variations is the wide-brimmed slouch hat, also known as a *saffa*, a practical form of headgear for jungle combat, though this was replaced on operational duties by a beret or by the standard British Army steel helmet. The green patch on the hat displays the Gurkha colours. By his side, he carries the fearsome kukri knife, a practical combat weapon in trained hands. Otherwise his uniform follows British lines, with khaki drill shirt, shorts, woollen socks and short puttees. The webbing is 1937-pattern, and the pouches hold magazines for his M1928 Thompson submachine gun.

Date:	December 1941
Unit:	9th Gurkha Rifles
Rank:	Corporal
Theatre:	Pacific
Location:	Malaya

Subedar-Major 20th Burma Rifles Indian Army Burma 1942

Here we see a Viceroy Commission Officer of the Indian Army, whose role would have been to advise British Army officers on issues relating to local soldiers and their welfare. The uniform is the British light-khaki service dress, smartly presented with an infantry officer's sword by his side, which featured a steel hilt and black leather scabbard, highly polished along with his Sam Browne belt and 1908-pattern webbing. Rank is displayed on the shoulder-straps, while the stand-and-fall collar of the tunic has regimental badges representing peacocks. The boots are the 'ammunition' type which were often worn by commandos and other special British Army units. During 1942 the Indian Army also became the recipients of a new jungle-green issue of combat clothing which went to British Army soldiers in the Far East theatre.

Date:	June 1942
Unit:	20th Burma Rifles
Rank:	Subedar-Major
Theatre:	Pacific
Location:	Burma

Lance-Corporal Royal Gurkha Rifles Indian Army Italy 1944

Gurkha units contributed impressively in Asian, African and European theatres during World War II. This soldier is in Italy as part of Indian Army forces shipped into the Mediterranean following heavy fighting in North Africa. The Gurkhas of the 4th Indian Division distinguished themselves at the battle of Monte Cassino, losing 3000 dead and injured in the process. This lance-corporal is clothed in the British Army temperate-zone battledress. However, rank markings colouration is different – here rifle-green – and the sleeve also bears the formation sign of the Indian Army. Over his uniform, the Gurkha has 1938-pattern British webbing in khaki, worn in battle-order configuration with just the backpack and ammunition pouches. The kukri sits in the back of the belt, and this soldier's weapon is the Thompson M1 submachine gun.

Date:	August 1944
Unit:	Royal Gurkha Rifles
Rank:	Lance-Corporal
Theatre:	Mediterranean
Location:	Italy

Lance-Corporal Indian Army Kashmir 1965

Even by the mid-1960s, the Indian Army was still very much indebted to its British colonial past in terms of its weaponry, dress and kit. The soldier here, who is a lance-corporal, is involved in one of the long-running conflicts between India and Pakistan over the disputed territory of Kashmir (these conflicts are still running today). His appearance is almost identical to that of Indian Army soldiers serving as British Empire forces during World War II. The light khaki shirt and battledress trousers are unadorned except for a single rank chevron on the sleeve. The webbing is British 1937-pattern with two utility/ammunition pouches for his .303 SMLE rifle. As a Sikh, this soldier wears the traditional turban, which has been dyed to match the uniform. The red band beneath the turban is known as the 'fifty', a name which indicates the fiftieth turn of the turban around the head.

Date:	1965
Unit:	Indian Army
Rank:	Lance-Corporal
Theatre:	Kashmir
Location:	Indo-Pakistan War

Private
Indian Army
Paratrooper
East Pakistan 1971

During India's invasion of East Pakistan in 1971 the Indian Army relied on its airborne forces to make rapid assaults and take the East Pakistan forces by surprise. Occupation of the region was achieved in only 12 days. This para has moved on from the khaki battledress of the 1960s, but the British influence remains, albeit in an updated form. He mostly wears British parachute clothing, including the Denison jump-smock in DPM (Disruptive Pattern Material) which features the white parachute, blue wings brevet on a khaki field. The helmet is also British para issue. Over the smock is the 1937-pattern webbing system, superseded by the 1958-pattern in the British Army, but still a good way of load-carrying. The pouches hold 30-round magazines for the 7.62mm (0.3in) L1A1 rifle, here with its short knife bayonet.

Date:	1971
Unit:	Indian Army
Rank:	Private
Theatre:	East Pakistan
Location:	Indo-Pakistan War

Marine
Marine Corps
Indonesian Navy
Borneo 1963

The Malayan 'Confrontation' in Borneo between 1963 and 1966 brought into conflict Indonesia – protesting against the formation of the Malaysian Federation – and British and Malaysian forces. The Marines were Indonesia's premier front-line troops. In dress, they owed much to the long-standing US presence in the Pacific region, as can be seen in the uniform (but not the firearm) of this Marine soldier. His steel helmet is the old US M1-pattern, covered in a dappled camouflage to match the rest of his uniform. This camouflage pattern – brown and olive-green patches on a light-green base – was a US camouflage used during the Pacific campaign in World War II. His webbing, US airborne issue from the 1950s, includes the 10-pouch ammunition belt originally designed for the M1 Garand rifle. The Czech Vz52 rifle features a folding bayonet.

Date:	1963
Unit:	Indonesian Marine Corps
Rank:	Marine
Theatre:	Borneo
Location:	Indonesian Confrontation

Private
Iranian Revolutionary
Guard Corps
Iran/Iraq Border 1980

The Iranian Revolutionary Guard Corps, also known as the *Pasdarin*, has been at the vanguard of Iran's armed operations for the last three decades, and consequently has seen massive losses. A horrific death toll during the eight-year war with neighbouring Iraq (1980–88) was something from which Iranian forces never completely recovered. Despite the decimation, however, the Revolutionary Guard still remains one of the Tehran regime's most capable resources. This soldier is pictured in 1980 at the beginning of hostilities with Iraq. The uniform of simple khaki fatigues is the same as that of the pre-revolutionary army, while the webbing is British in type, the helmet the US M1, and the weapon the German Heckler & Koch G3. The mix of sources shown here indicates the supply difficulties always experienced by Iran.

Date:	1980
Unit:	Iranian Revolutionary Guard Corps
Rank:	Private
Theatre:	Iran/Iraq border
Location:	Gulf War 1980–88

Corporal
Iraqi Army
Shatt al Arab
Waterway 1980

The Iraqi Army's heavy losses in the First Gulf War (1980–88) were compounded by the Gulf War of 1990–91, in which tens of thousands of Iraqi soldiers were slaughtered under Allied air assaults. This soldier shows the typical khaki fatigues of the Iraqi troops at the beginning of the 1980s. Iraqi uniforms were of low quality, yet this soldier wears desert boots of canvas and rubber, far better in the desert temperatures than the black leather boots worn by many soldiers. Insignia in Iraqi forces tends to be fairly inconspicuous. This soldier has a black sleeve chevron to indicate his rank (officers would display rank in yellow or gold on an epaulette slide), while the black beret features a national emblem, a gold eagle. The webbing belt's leather pouch holds the AKMS assault rifle's magazine. The Kalashnikov is the standard Iraqi weapon.

Date:	1980
Unit:	Iraqi Army
Rank:	Corporal
Location:	Shatt al Arab Waterway
Conflict:	Gulf War

Irregular Palmach Infantry Palestine 1948

Israel's history of conflict began even during the very acts of its creation in 1948 as it emerged from the contentious UN partition of Palestine into Jewish and Arab territories. Jewish and Arab citizens in these territories formed themselves into irregular armies to fight a vicious, unconventional war, which eventually became a mass Arab assault upon the fledgling Jewish nation. The main Israeli defence force was the Haganah, the Palmach being an excellent infantry force within the Haganah which brought with it much combat experience from World War II. The Palmach had to equip themselves with whatever war surplus was to hand. This soldier has a US drill shirt matched with British drill trousers; the webbing is a US Army cartridge belt and the water canteen has an M1910 cover. Armament in this case is the 7.92mm (0.311in) Model 24, which was a Czech copy of the German Kar 98k rifle.

Date:	1948
Unit:	Palmach Infantry
Rank:	Irregular
Location:	Palestine/Israel
Conflict:	Israeli War of Independence

Private
Sayeret Golani
Mount Hermon 1967

The *Sayeret Golani* are an élite reconnaissance and combat unit within the regular Golani Brigade of the Israeli Army. Training for the unit – as for all élite units of the Israeli Army – is tough to the extreme, and the soldier pictured here will have undergone nearly two years of training before being allowed to enter it. Israeli military units are very visually relaxed in nature, often tending slightly towards informality and therefore keeping rank and insignia to a minimum. This soldier is pictured during Israel's lightning Six-Day War of 1967, in operation against Syrian forces on Mount Hermon. He wears an olive-green Israeli 'battledress' zippered jacket, with 'lizard' pattern camouflage trousers commonly seen on élite Israeli troops (though the regular olive-green outfits are more common). The webbing is US issue and the rifle he carries is a heavy-barrelled support version of the FN FAL rifle.

Date:	1967
Unit:	*Sayeret Golani*
Rank:	Private
Location:	Mount Hermon
Conflict:	Six-Day War

First Lieutenant Israeli Armoured Corps Sinai 1967

The Six-Day War was a primary test for Israeli's tactical abilities in multi-arm warfare, and it passed with exemplary performance. Israeli air power decimated opposing air forces before they were airborne; Israel's 800 British Centurion and US M4 tanks dominated the open battlefields. This Israeli tank commander is shown in full communications gear, the effective coordination of the Main Battle Tank formations being one of the vital ingredients of the Israeli success. His vented and padded helmet is of US World War II type, made of fibre and leather. Into this helmet are built receivers in the ear pieces and a boom-arm microphone; the junction box for the communications system can be seen on his chest. Apart from this, he carries only a revolver and a water bottle. Rank is indicated on the shoulder-straps.

Date:	1967
Unit:	Israeli Armoured Corps
Rank:	First Lieutenant
Theatre:	Sinai
Location:	Six-Day War

Crewman Aeromedical Evacuation Unit Sinai 1973

Aeromedical Evacuation Units (AEUs) provide battlefield medical rescue and combat first aid, but they are also skilled combat soldiers. During the Yom Kippur War in 1973, they performed numerous evacuations from the battlefronts, getting most soldiers to medical help within half an hour of evacuation. The uniform of these units in the 1970s was a copy of the US K2B flight suit in olive-green. This was a one-piece overall with large, zippered pockets and elasticated ankles. It was held at the waist with a simple web belt, and pistols and water bottles were usually the only types of equipment carried on the body. Helmet types varied, including single-visored models such as the HGU-26 and SPH-4C. The helmet featured here is genuine US Army: the CVC 'bone-dome' is made of ballistic nylon and features a foldable boom mike.

Date:	1973
Unit:	Unit 669 Aeromedical Evacuation Unit
Rank:	Crewman
Location:	Sinai
Conflict:	Yom Kippur War

Corporal 202nd Parachute Brigade Lebanon 1982

This Israeli soldier patrolling in the Lebanon is wearing the standard olive-green field uniform of the Israeli Defence Force (IDF), capped by a ballistic-nylon helmet that acted as the replacement for the old steel variety. The webbing is also Israeli issue, and can be distinguished from foreign supply by the 'boot-lace' fittings connecting the straps to the belt. What is more notable about this soldier is his weaponry as, prepared for the dangerous possibilities of a street patrol in the Lebanon, he carries a 5.56mm (0.22in) Galil assault rifle, produced in Israel in response to disatisfaction with Israeli small arms during the Yom Kippur War, and an excellent, reliable weapon with a bolt-action based on the Kalashnikov rifles. The soldier carries IMI bullet-trap rifle-grenades for the Galil, most likely with high explosive or tear-gas warheads for urban combat.

Date:	1982
Unit:	202nd Parachute Brigade
Rank:	Corporal
Location:	South Lebanon
Conflict:	Israeli invasion of Lebanon

First Lieutenant
Sayeret Tzanhanim
Lebanon 1985

The *Sayeret Tzanhanim* is the élite reconnaissance arm of the Israeli parachute brigade, and specializes in all aspects of reconnaissance, including parachute and armoured insertion. This soldier evidently belongs to an armoured deployment, as clearly indicated by the Type 602 crewman's helmet, a copy of US designs, containing full communications headset and made of the exceptionally tough kevlar material (earlier versions were manufactured in ballistic nylon). He is most likely a crewmember aboard an M113 Armoured Personnel Vehicle, a US APC bought in large numbers not only by Israel, but over 40 countries world-wide. The M113 was used extensively for urban reconnaissance in the Lebanon. The uniform is a winter issue called the *Beged Horef*, a one-piece overall with insulated padding, usually worn underneath combat waterproof jackets. Rank is displayed on the shoulder-straps.

Date:	1985
Unit:	Sayeret Tzanhanim
Rank:	First Lieutenant
Location:	Lebanon
Conflict:	Arab/Israeli Wars

Private
202nd Parachute Brigade
Gaza Strip 1990s

The 202nd Parachute Brigade, formed in 1955 as an élite airborne wing of the Israeli Defence Force, has fought in conventional battles and counter-terrorist operations. This soldier is on patrol in Israeli-occupied territory, his olive-drab uniform showing the Israeli soldier in his current form, though here the uniform is worn over kevlar body armour to protect against small-arm rounds and shell splinter. Further protective gears includes the ballistic nylon helmet. Insignia is at a minimum, though the paras often wear silver parachute wings over the left breast to indicate their airborne status. The helmet is occasionally replaced by the regimental red beret – awarded after five properly executed static-line jumps – even on combat duties. This soldier carries the US M16A2 with the M203 40mm (1.57in) grenade-launcher attachment.

Date:	1990s
Unit:	202nd Parachute Brigade
Rank:	Private
Location:	Gaza Strip
Conflict:	Arab/Israeli Wars

Corporal
Milizia Volontaria Per La Sicurezza
Sicily 1940

The *Milizia Volontaria Per La Sicurezza* was Mussolini's fascist militia organization – also known as Blackshirts – which, from its formation in 1922, rose to a strength of 177 Legions and 200 battalions in 1940. The Roman 'Legion' name was due to Mussolini's creation of the Blackshirts around Roman military structures, Roman symbolism representing the new martial values of fascism. A total of 39 of the Legions were attached to the Italian Army, as is the case with this soldier who wears standard grey-green Italian Army uniform. His unit is distinguished by black additions to the uniform, including his black tie and shirt beneath the tunic, and also black collar patches featuring the fascist fascio, a representation of an axe bound by rods, signifying the fascist 'strength through unity' message. The dagger is a special Blackshirt design.

Date:	January 1940
Unit:	MVSN
Rank:	Corporal
Theatre:	Mediterranean
Location:	Sicily

Air Marshal Italo Balbo Italian Air Force North Africa 1940

Air Marshal Italo Balbo is seen here in what is essentially Italian Army uniform. This is due to the fact that at this time, the air force and army shared much in way of their uniform styles. The tunic belongs to the tropical dress, while the breeches are those which would have been used for the temperate dress. True to the officer class, he wears a pair of riding boots. His rank is displayed in two locations: firstly, his shoulder boards; and secondly, his peaked cap. The cap features the greca embroidered section worn by generals and field marshals, with a cap badge that features eagle, laurel wreath and Royal Crown. Officers of Balbo's rank also had a purple-red backing under the badge. Other insignia worn by Balbo includes a pilot-qualification badge which is positioned on the left breast just above the row of decoration ribbons.

Date:	May 1940
Unit:	Italian Air Force
Rank:	Air Marshal
Theatre:	Mediterranean
Location:	North Africa

Major
One Group
Italian Air Force
Libya 1940

Despite its bulky appearance and its colouration, the flying uniform pictured here is actually a summer uniform. This one-piece overall was made of white linen and featured a distinctive cross-over breast. It is worn here with a matching padded crash helmet, also of linen. This uniform was also available as a two-piece outfit, and in both cases the rank markings were situated on the cuffs in gold lace. The only other insignia which can be seen here is worn as a squadron badge on the left breast. During the winter months, the uniform would not alter at all in style; however, its colour would be changed to an olive-green, and it would also feature a padded lining. This lieutenant is seen during the early Italian operations in Libya, though by the end of 1940, the air force was suffering from severe losses as well as deficits in both parts and fuel.

Date:	June 1940
Unit:	One Group
Rank:	Major
Theatre:	Mediterranean
Location:	Libya

Colonel
36th Infantry
Regiment
France 1940

Italian officer uniforms were of excellent cut and quality. In essence the basic officer uniform was the same as that of the general ranks, yet the colour was lighter than the grey-green of lower ranks, and the twill cloth was of better quality. The colonel here is shown in his cordellino uniform with a vivid display of rank, arm-of-service, and decorations. The tunic itself features the rank on the collar patches and in the stripes on the forearm made of gold braid. The narrower stripes give the rank itself, while the thicker stripe indicates senior rank in general. The colonel's decorations appear extensive. The two most visible – a gold eagle and crown and swords – indicate war academy graduation and promotion through active service. The cap features two badges, the red backing referring to the colonel's status as a regimental commander.

Date:	June 1940
Unit:	36th Infantry Regiment
Rank:	Colonel
Theatre:	Mediterranean
Location:	Southern France

Corporal
VI Eritrea Battalion
Italian Colonial Army
Ethiopia 1940

The Italian Colonial Army formed a large part of the Italian Army's overseas contingent, particularly in the African theatre where Italy had several colonies. Italy's East African Army alone had some 200,000 colonial troops compared to 88,000 Italians. The soldier here is a corporal in the VI Eritrea Battalion, the unit identified by the green tassel on the tarbusc hat. The uniform is ideal wear for the African climate, and it was established as a pattern for colonial forces in 1929. Its white colouration restricts heat build-up in the clothing, and both the tunic and the trousers are loose-fitting for good ventilation. The only markings on the tunic are the rank chevrons on the arm, the three stars signifying 10 years service. Over this he wears khaki leather Italian Army webbing which holds four ammunition pouches for his Mannlicher-Carcano M91/38 rifle.

Date:	June 1940
Unit:	VI Eritrea Battalion
Rank:	Corporal
Theatre:	Africa
Location:	Ethiopia

Lieutenant
Italian Army
Sidi Azeis 1940

Italian forces had some of the best desert clothing of the war, cut for comfort and durability in the caustic climate of North and Central Africa. This lieutenant is wearing a light khaki drill uniform, consisting of a sahariana jacket, shorts, long socks and suede boots. He also wears a bustina field cap with the flaps undone to provide shade from the sun for the neck. Some care is needed when identifying Italian rank, as all ranks had the silver savoy collar stars seen here. Actual rank for officer was confined to the shoulder-straps; here two stars for the rank of lieutenant (the higher rank of first lieutenant had a single bar). Apart from these features, the only other insignia is the cap badge, which depicts a gold hand-grenade inset with the regimental number. A good testimony to the comfort of this uniform was that both the British and German soldiers were quick to wear the sahariana if they could obtain supplies.

Date:	August 1940
Unit:	Infantry Division
Rank:	Lieutenant
Theatre:	Mediterranean
Location:	Sidi Azeis

Tankman
Ariete Division
Italian Army
North Africa 1941

The Italian Army suffered a chronic downscaling of its armoured resources as the war went on, mainly because Italian tanks could not compete with Allied technologies. From an initial three divisions at the beginning of the war, by 1943 this was down to one division, only reviving to two divisions once Italy had swapped sides following the 1943 armistice. Here we see a soldier of the Ariete Division, one of four armoured divisions which existed in World War II: *Ariete*, *Littorio*, *Centauro* and *Giovanni Fascisti*. His uniform is that of a tank crewmember, with khaki tunic and trousers covered by a three-quarter length leather coat, and a crash helmet with neck protector. No markings are visible, but from 1940 onwards collar patches are seen, with flames on a dark-blue background. Overall design of this outfit copies that of French armoured crews.

Date:	January 1941
Unit:	*Ariete* Division
Rank:	Tankman
Theatre:	Mediterranean
Location:	North Africa

Corporal
Gruppi Sahariana
North Africa 1942

*G*ruppi Sahariana* soldiers were some of the best of Italy's colonial forces. Their intimacy with the North African environment, plus a courageous disposition, combined to make them excellent fighters. Yet their skills could not prevent the crushing Italian defeats of the early 1940s, during which Italy lost around 200,000 men (including POWs) to British offensives. This corporal of the *Gruppi Sahariana* wears an Italian Army white full-dress jacket with khaki sirical trousers and a webbing belt with three long, leather pouches (these pouches were sometimes arranged on a bandolier for mounted or motorized soldiers). The sash wrapped around his waist is an arm-of-service colour, here indicating the 3rd Service Group, while the rank is displayed as a single red chevron; rank markings like those shown here were only used after Italian nationality had been granted to Libyan citizens in 1939.

Date:	January 1942
Unit:	*Gruppi Sahariana*
Rank:	Corporal
Theatre:	Mediterranean
Location:	North Africa

Sergeant-Major Italian Marine Infantry Sicily 1942

Notwithstanding the blue-and-white navy collar, Italian Marine soldiers had little to distinguish them visually from the regular army, though the grey-green jumper which is worn here with matching pantaloons and puttees was usually blue in colour when issued to army troops. However, in the North African theatre, the jumper also came in khaki to match the light khaki drill uniform worn by all Italian soldiers in that particular front (though the jumper there had a rectangular collar with two white stripes down the border). However, a common denominator in these uniforms was bright-red collar- or cuff patches, and these depicted the lion of St Mark embroidered in yellow thread or rendered in gilt metal. An interesting feature of this soldier's uniform is the British webbing which was manufactured by the Mills Company.

Date:	February 1942
Unit:	Italian Marine Infantry
Rank:	Sergeant-Major
Theatre:	Mediterranean
Location:	Sicily

Ranking Lieutenant Taranto Command Italian Navy Mediterranean 1942

At the outbreak of World War II, the Italian Navy fielded an impressive fleet of over 300 combat vessels (including 6 battleships) and, by August 1943, 259,000 personnel. However, its contribution to Axis combat efforts was fairly minimal. Its greatest achievements lay in dangerous resupply missions to Italian troops across the British-dominated Mediterranean. This officer of the Taranto command wears the blue reefer jacket and matching trousers and peaked cap, the standard dress of Italian Navy officers. The cap badge is the Italian naval insignia: an oval shield bracketed by laurel leaves and surmounted by a crown, all in gold embroidery. Rank is shown on the navy-blue shoulder-straps (more senior officers would have their straps outlined in gold embroidery), and on the cuffs, the silver stars on the collar being common to all ranks.

Date:	June 1942
Unit:	Taranto Command
Rank:	Ranking Lieutenant
Theatre:	Mediterranean
Location:	Mediterranean Sea

Captain 184th Parachute Division Tunisia 1942

I taly was one of the earliest pioneers of military parachute forces, forming an experimental para unit in 1927 and formalized para companies by 1938. The captain here is seen in a new style of para uniform, introduced in 1942. While the camouflage patterning seems to allude to the ochre, green and mustard shades of the British Denison smock, the jacket is actually a combination of an Italian Army field tunic with the long sahariana. The trousers were plain khaki and could be fastened at the ankle for a tight fit when jumping. Here they are also seen with a pair of leather-padded knee-protectors. The steel para helmet featured a forked chin-and-neck strap for maximum support. The webbing, pouches and map case are all standard Italian Army issue. The firearm is the Beretta M38A submachine gun, common within élite units of the Italian forces.

Date:	December 1942
Unit:	184th Parachute Division
Rank:	Captain
Theatre:	Mediterranean
Location:	Tunisia

Seaman Italian Social Republic Navy Italy 1944

This soldier's uniform, pictured in late 1944, had already undergone some of the significant changes which were imposed following the effective switch of sides by the Italians in September 1943. The actual pattern of pre- and post-fascist uniform stayed roughly the same: a navy-blue 'square rig' uniform worn with either a sailor's cap, a steel helmet (as seen here), or a peaked cap for officer ranks. The real changes lay in the insignia, which now reflected a more neutral and less belligerent ideology. On the peaked cap, out went the crown from the badge and in came a winged bird, and the embroidered-gold rings on the cap band also went, to be replaced by a blue-and-gold chin cord for lieutenants and a gold cord for higher ranks. Affecting all sailors, the gladio replaced the silver savoy stars which previously featured on the collar of all ranks' tunics.

Date:	October 1944
Unit:	Italian Social Republic Navy
Rank:	Seaman
Theatre:	Mediterranean
Location:	Northern Italy

Sergeant-Major *Folgore* Brigade Lebanon 1982

This sergeant-major of the *Paracadutisti Folgore* is one element of the 2000-strong Italian military group which acted as peacekeepers in Beruit in the early 1980s. This was just one of many Italian peacekeeping roles in the Middle East under United Nations' commitments. The one-piece jump uniform, in a camouflage similar to that of the British Denison smock, has its roots in Italian World War II para tunics, featuring elasticated ankles and reinforced and padded shoulders and knees. This para wears the red beret of paras world-wide, with a parachute/laurel-leaf badge. The silver savoy collar stars, removed after the Italian armistice in 1943, are returned. The boots are thickly soled to prevent slippage inside an aircraft. His Italian-made weaponry is the Beretta BM-59 Ital para rifle with folding stock and, in the holster, the Beretta Model 92 pistol.

Date:	1982
Unit:	*Folgore* Brigade
Rank:	Sergeant-Major
Location:	Beirut
Conflict:	Peacekeeping operations, Lebanon

Private Italian *Alpini* North Italy 1990s

The *Alpini* is the Italian Army's élite mountain force, consisting of a high percentage of indigenous Alpine inhabitants. It exists in five brigade formations: *Tridentina, Orobica, Iuwa, Cadore, Tauninense*. This soldier is wearing the camouflage shirt and trousers worn by *Alpini* soldiers during the summer. It features reinforced elbow- and knee sections for climbing, and tightly elasticated ankles which are covered by a calf-high pair of rubber climbing boots. Though the *Alpini* wear the silver savoy collar stars of the regular Italian Army – the stars represent the birthplace of the Italian Army in the Kingdom of Sardinia-Piedmont – they also wear green collar patches. In winter, the uniform becomes an all-white snowsuit, with specially adapted gloves to allow the operation of weapons such as the Beretta BM59, seen here.

Date:	1990s
Unit:	Italian *Alpini*
Rank:	Private
Location:	North Italy
Conflict:	None

Officer *Nucleo Operativo Centrale* Milan 1990s

The *Nucleo Operativo Centrale* is Italy's primary counter-terrorist and hostage-rescue force, trained along similar lines as the SAS Counter-Revolutionary Warfare team. This officer dons a uniform utilized by many HR units world-wide when operating in urban constraints. His dark overalls give some measure of camouflage within a smoke-filled building interior, and his trousers also have fastenings at the ankle to stop them snagging when fast-roping (the harness and equipment for fast-roping is seen at the waist). Fire-retardant overalls reduce the risk of burn injuries. Protection comes from a kevlar flak jacket and visored helmet made from kevlar or ballistic nylon. All his weaponry is Italian produced: a 9mm Beretta Model 12S submachine gun, and a Beretta Model 84 pistol tucked in his belt in case of weapon jams.

Date:	1990s
Unit:	*Nucleo Operativo Centrale*
Rank:	Officer
Location:	Milan
Conflict:	None

160

Marine San Marco Battalion Italy 1990s

The San Marco Battalion forms a specialist sub-section of the Italian Marines which is trained in élite methods of multi-theatre operations, rather like the US Navy SEALs. All are parachute-trained and some of the best soldiers join the élite naval incursion group known as the *Demolitori Ostacoli Antisbarco* (Shore Demolition Group). This soldier is in winter training in the mountainous regions of North Italy, with a three-quarter length ski jacket belted at the waist with an Italian-issue web belt. Beneath this he is wearing the standard Italian Army camouflage combat uniform. His boots have canvas uppers, thus reducing possibilities of frostbite or trench foot. He is heavily armed with an MG42/59, a post-war update of the World War II German MG42, which is now standard issue to Italian and Austrian armies as a unit-support weapon.

Date:	1990s
Unit:	San Marco Battalion
Rank:	Marine
Location:	North Italy
Conflict:	None

Private Imperial Japanese Army Luzon 1941

This soldier is wearing the typical cotton khaki dress of a Japanese soldier in the tropical theatres of World War II. However, he is without the single-breasted khaki jacket with stand-and-fall collar which was introduced in 1938, and which replaced an earlier jacket with a stiff collar. The pantaloons were usually bound to the knee with khaki tapes, these being a fairly sensible measure when walking upon the insect-covered jungle floors of tropical Asia. As headgear, he wears the standard Japanese Army field cap, with a chin-strap of brown leather and a removable neck sunguard. The cap could be worn beneath the Japanese steel helmet. Because of the temperatures in the Pacific theatre, it is uncommon to see the Japanese greatcoats; the M90 was single-breasted and the M98 had a double-breasted style.

Date:	December 1941
Unit:	Imperial Japanese Army
Rank:	Private
Theatre:	Pacific
Location:	Luzon

Senior NCO Indian National Army Malaysia 1942

Though this soldier is an Indian national, he falls under the auspices of the Japanese Army as a member of the anti-British Indian National Army (INA). The INA was a unit put together mainly from Indian POWs (head of recruitment was General Mohan Singh, previously of the 14th Punjab Regiment) captured by the Japanese amongst surrendering colonial forces in places like Singapore. Reasons for joining ran from a genuine hostility towards British rule in India or because many POWs were eager to escape prison conditions. The senior NCO pictured here retains the khaki field-drill uniform of the Indian Army, though Japanese uniforms were also sometimes worn. There is little to identify him as an INA soldier; only company and field officers had the letters 'INA' on their shoulder-straps beneath their rank markings.

Date:	September 1942
Unit:	Indian National Army
Rank:	Senior NCO
Theatre:	Pacific
Location:	Malaysia

Paratrooper Naval Parachute Troops Pacific 1941

The soldier here is seen wearing the olive-drab jump overall issued to all naval paratroopers. It was worn over a matching shirt and pantaloons, though it could be worn on its own. One of the most interesting features is the helmet, which is a Japanese Army para pattern in steel but fitted with a canvas cover for camouflage. This was not the only helmet available: naval and army paras also wore leather helmets (though these were replaced by the steel version as war progressed) and even imported German para helmets. All naval helmets featured the anchor motif at the front. German influence can be seen in the overall design of the uniform, particularly in the high-boots with rubber soles. No weaponry is carried here, but typically a soldier would jump with a M2 7.7mm (0.31in) paratroop rifle, about four hand-grenades, and ammunition.

Date:	December 1941
Unit:	Japanese Navy
Rank:	Private
Theatre:	Pacific
Location:	Pacific Ocean

Rating
Combined Fleet
Japanese Navy
Philippine Sea 1942

This style of white rig uniform was worn by sailors who were undertaking administrative or service roles aboard a ship or at land installations. It consists of a simple white tunic and trousers, all loose-fitting, worn with a pair of black leather shoes. Markings and insignia are minimal. The cap features a blue naval anchor and also a single blue band held in place by a strap. This band signalled that the soldier is a rating, whereas officers' caps would have two blue bands and also a gold anchor surrounded by a gold wreath (note, however, that the colour of the anchor might be varied, depending on the colour of the cap). The only other badge on this rating's uniform is that of Musician 3rd Class, visible distinguished in blue on his left sleeve. A short-sleeved version of this uniform was available for servicemen in different theatres.

Date:	May 1942
Unit:	Combined Fleet
Rank:	Rating
Theatre:	Pacific
Location:	Philippine Sea

Lieutenant 5th Fleet Japanese Navy Tokyo 1943

Japanese Navy uniforms were typically understated, as is the case here with this lieutenant of the 5th Fleet. He is seen in his regulation whites, composed of a single-breasted stand-collar tunic with five gold buttons and side-slash pockets, matching trousers and white leather shoes. This uniform contrasts with the standard service uniform which was of the same cut but came in a blue cloth and was worn with black shoes. The lieutenant's rank is on the shoulder-straps, but officer rank in the Japanese Navy could also be distinguished by a black silver lace edging the collar, the pockets and the tunic hem. On the shoulder-straps, the gold stripes set the general class of rank, while the stars identified the specific rank. Other rank markings were often placed on the cuffs, in gold on the blue dress uniform, and black on the service dress and whites.

Date:	February 1943
Unit:	5th Fleet
Rank:	Lieutenant
Theatre:	Pacific
Location:	Tokyo

Private Jordanian Army West Jordan 1967

This soldier is seen during Israel's victorious Six-Day War of 1967, probably Jordan's most traumatic military episode this century, which saw it lose over 6000 troops and in which its air and armour forces were devastated beyond recovery. His uniform is a mix of items from various other nations, a combination which signifies the problems in logistics and economy in Jordan. The actual uniform shirt and trousers – made in an olive-drab herringbone twill – are Jordanian-made, though the style alludes to US World War II combat dress from later in the conflict in the European and Pacific theatres. However, the British influence in Jordanian history is apparent in the British Army Mk 1 steel helmet with camouflage cover, while the 1937-pattern webbing is also of British manufacture. The weapon is US – the M1 Garand – and ammunition for this is carried in British battle-order pouches on the belt.

Date:	1967
Unit:	Jordanian Army
Rank:	Private
Theatre:	West Jordan
Location:	Six-Day War

Private
Azad Kashmir Army
Kashmir 1950

The *Azad* ('Free') *Kashmir* Army was essentially a revolutionary army. Its objective within Kashmir was the establishment of a Muslim rule in accord with the majority faith of Kashmir's people. In this it was supported by Pakistan, but even so, the *Azad Kashmir* forces were never strong enough to make the impact required. As we would expect, the *Azad Kashmir* soldiers would dress and equip themselves from a variety of local and international sources, though there is some standardization in the use of Pakistani supplies, which in turn were much derived from Indian sources. This soldier wears Indian Army cavalry dress from pre-independence India, consisting of a long, heavy tunic and trousers. His headgear is a simple beret with unit colours, but turbans are also common. The rifle is the British .303in (7.7mm) Lee Enfield Mk III, the dominant army weapon of the Indian subcontinent during the turbulent post-war years.

Date:	1950
Unit:	*Azad Kashmir* Army
Rank:	Private
Location:	Kashmir
Conflict:	Kashmir Independence War

Private Korean People's Army Pyongyang 1950

In contrast to many United Nations troops in the early years of the Korean War, this soldier is extremely well-dressed for the severe Korean winter climate. His jacket and trousers are made from thickly quilted material, the jacket featuring a double-breasted design with zipper fastening to reduce penetration by wind chill. The hat is similarly judicious, as the earflaps would have prevented the frostbite that afflicted many troops in the sub-zero winter months. Note the complete absence of rank or markings on this cold-weather gear; the normal uniform – based on Soviet patterns – would have rank on the shoulder-straps and the collar. The Soviet weapon is a 7.62mm (0.3in) PPSh41, here fitted with a 71-round drum magazine. Though this soldier is well equipped, a North Korean soldier's life was one of terrible austerity.

Date:	1950
Unit:	Korean People's Army
Rank:	Private
Location:	Near Pyongyang
Conflict:	Korean War

Private Army of the Republic of Korea South Korea 1951

South Korea's Army lost around 45 per cent of all its troops in the first three months of the Korean War, such was the state of its structure, equipment and morale. UN military support and US equipment saved it from an even more ignominious fate at the hands of the North Koreans. This soldier shows his indebtedness to the US in particular. His clothing is the US M1943 battledress, a uniform which worked on a layering system. The outer layers had good properties of wind- and rain-resistance, while inner layers supported warmth. Such a uniform gave fairly substantial winter-weather protection. The US M1 helmet is worn on top of a woollen cap and the weapon is the US .30in M1 Carbine, here fitted with an M4 bayonet. US supplies to the South Korean Army improved as the war went on, and tilted the war steadily in South Korea's favour.

Date:	1951
Unit:	Army of the Republic of Korea
Rank:	Private
Location:	South Korea
Conflict:	Korean War

Trooper
UN Partisan Infantry
North Korea 1952

The UN Partisan Infantry was around 22,000 strong and fought a vigorous and effective guerrilla war against the North Korean regime from within North Korea itself. It was made up of individuals highly motivated against the Communist system, and with copious US backing (this came to the UNPI as the US slowly realized its worth), it achieved considerable impact, mainly in drawing North Korean troops away from the front line and killing some 69,000 of them. By 1952 the US logistics train to the UNPI was in full swing, as is evident by the elements of this soldier's dress and equipment. The uniform is US World War II surplus; the shirt is from the herringbone-twill jungle dress issued to US troops in the Pacific theatre, and this is worn with a pair of matching olive-green combat trousers and cap. A US M1936 web belt supports a leather pistol holster, which contains the classic Browning 9mm pistol.

Date:	1952
Unit:	United Nations Partisan Infantry
Rank:	Trooper
Location:	North Korea
Conflict:	Korean War

171

Private
RoK Capital Division
Vietnam 1969

The RoK contributed over 47,000 troops to the Allied cause during the Vietnam War, sending mainly its élite units such as the RoK Capital Division, known as the 'Tigers' after their divisional badge (a roaring tiger head on a green shield, worn as a shoulder patch). The areas controlled by Korean troops became some of the best-controlled regions of South Vietnam, and the Viet Cong lived in fear of being captured by Korean troops, who had a justifiable reputation for ruthless killing and torture. The most striking element of this soldier's dress is the camouflage, actually a Korean version of the foliage patterns used by certain US units in the Pacific in World War II. Over this he wears a US-issue M1955 flak vest, while for headgear he has a US M1 helmet with matching camouflage cover. He wears the US canvas and leather jungle boots; these proved superior to pure leather boots, which rotted in the humidity.

Date:	1969
Unit:	RoK Capital Division
Rank:	Private
Location:	South Vietnam
Conflict:	Vietnam War

Private
Army of the
Republic of Korea
Korean Border 1990s

The South Korean Army has become one of the world's more modern fighting forces, investing heavily in military hardware and training on account of continual border tensions with its Communist neighbour to the north. Most of its military expenditure is directed to the profit of the US, still a major presence in the region. This soldier shows the latest US combat gear. The uniform shirt and trousers are of South Korean manufacture, yet the camouflage is directly borrowed from the modern US M81 Woodland pattern. His kevlar helmet is the US PASGT (Personal Armor System, Ground Troops) system, known as the 'Fritz' helmet due to its resemblance to World War II German helmets. The webbing is the US ALICE type, and the rifle is the 5.56mm (0.22in) M16A2, the current version of the M16 in service with the US forces.

Date:	1990s
Unit:	Army of the Republic of Korea
Rank:	Private
Location:	Korean Border
Conflict:	None

Private Lebanese Army Beirut 1982

The Lebanese Army in the early 1980s was a force in constant action. Militia forces within its own borders meant incessant counter-terrorist operations, and the Israeli invasion in 1982 gave these militias (particularly the Druze and Shi'ite Amal groups) the opportunity to impose a serious defeat upon the army from which it never recovered. Despite the close ties of the US to Israel, the Lebanon had received much US military support and investment in the 1970s. This soldier, caught up in the street-fighting in Beirut that ravaged the city in the 1980s, is carrying a US M16A1 rifle with plentiful ammunition in Lebanese Army web pouches on the belt (the sling on the M16 is a custom attachment). Uniform is plain olive-green fatigues and unit/rank insignia is entirely absent: logos and badges could have terrible consequences for the soldier if he was captured by one of the militias.

Date:	1982
Unit:	Lebanese Army
Rank:	Private
Location:	Beirut
Conflict:	Lebanese Civil War/ Israeli Invasion

Guerrilla Malayan Races Liberation Army Rural Malaya 1953

This soldier of the Malayan Races Independence Army (MRLA) – a revolutionary army fighting for self-government against British rule in the 1950s – in most respects resembles a Japanese soldier of World War II. This is partly due to the massive stocks of Japanese clothing and equipment left over in South-east Asia after Japanese occupation, though the MRLA often produced its own clothing to the Japanese style rather than simply appropriating existing stocks. The khaki shirt and trousers are Japanese in style, and like Japanese Army uniform, the trousers are gathered up into knee-high khaki tapes. A five-pouch ammunition bandolier is worn over the shirt, this being British 1937-pattern to go with the .303in (7.7mm) Lee Enfield No.1 Mk III rifle. Instead of a rank denotation, this soldier has a red Communist star on his cap.

Date:	1953
Unit:	Malayan Races Liberation Army
Rank:	Guerrilla
Location:	Rural Malaya
Conflict:	Malayan 'Emergency'

Lieutenant-Colonel Cyclist Regiment Dutch Army Holland 1940

The pattern of uniform worn by the lieutenant-colonel was introduced into the Dutch Army in 1912. It features a grey-green tunic and trousers, with black leather riding boots (only for officers and mounted soldiers; others wore black ankle boots) and side cap, though this style of cap was actually introduced in 1937 instead of the traditional kepi. The tunic itself is single-breasted with four large patch pockets and seven bronze buttons at the front. The stand collar displays the rank – two stars and a bar for the rank of lieutenant-colonel – with the circular badge by the side being the spoked wheel of the cycle regiment and the blue piping indicating the arm-of-service (infantry). This blue piping is also repeated down the seam of the trousers. His leather webbing is of Dutch issue and features a compass pouch and a pistol over on his right hip.

Date:	April 1940
Unit:	Cyclist Regiment
Rank:	Lieutenant-Colonel
Theatre:	North-west Europe
Location:	Holland

2nd Lieutenant Fighter Squadron Dutch Air Force Holland 1940

Distinguishing a Dutch airman from a member of the Dutch ground forces can be difficult at initial glance, as the air force was classed as part of the army and thus donned the same grey-green tunic, pantaloons and boots. The arm-of-service piping around the collar and the cuffs is also blue, but of a lighter hue than the infantry. Insignia and other markings are what set the air force apart. The tunic has air-force wings over the left breast pocket (also featuring on the greatcoat and the French double-breasted leather coat worn as a flying jacket), while the collar has the rank star and engine-and-propeller badges in gold. His headgear is distinctive: he is wearing the kepi, something which began to be replaced in the Dutch forces in 1937, and was rarely found from 1940. This uniform is privately made from an expensive whipcord cloth.

Date:	May 1940
Unit:	Fighter Squadron
Rank:	2nd Lieutenant
Theatre:	North-west Europe
Location:	Holland

Private Dutch Army Indonesia 1946

Like many European countries after World War II, the Netherlands was economically crippled by the conflict. As a result, the Dutch forces which went immediately into action to fight the independence movement of the Dutch East Indies were clothed and equipped mainly in war surplus. The camouflage jungle overall is actually of US derivation, and was the type used by US soldiers during the Pacific campaign. The overall featured a more involved approach to camouflage through the introduction of foliage patterns. Headgear is mixed: a US olive-green fatigue cap, topped by a British Mk 1 steel helmet, this latter item being matched by British 1937-pattern web equipment. The submachine gun is also British, the 9mm Lanchester, a Rolls-Royce of submachine guns, which was manufactured for the Royal Navy in small numbers. This private has attached the long Lee-Enfield bayonet to his gun.

Date:	1946
Unit:	Dutch Army
Rank:	Private
Location:	Indonesia
Conflict:	Indonesian Independence War

Corporal Royal Netherlands Marine Corps Netherlands 1970s

The Royal Netherlands Marine Corps is an élite force within the Dutch military which, in addition to the usual land-based and amphibious roles provided by any Marine force, provides counter-terrorist and hostage-rescue training to a exemplary few, though this means extending training by a tough 48 weeks. This soldier is more than likely undergoing that training, as his Uzi 9mm submachine gun is essentially a close-quarter weapon. He wears standard army dress for the Dutch land forces: olive-green trousers with a heavy matching pullover, this featuring reinforced elbow patches. Over the top is worn a flak jacket. The webbing system and helmet are both US: the helmet is the M1 and the web belt is the M1967 model. Kit includes a haversack for grenades and munitions explosives, a water bottle, and a holster for a Browning pistol.

Date:	1970s
Unit:	Royal Netherlands Marine Corps
Rank:	Corporal
Location:	Netherlands
Conflict:	None

179

Lieutenant Infantry Division Norwegian Army Norway 1940

Like the forces of the Netherlands, the Norwegian Army adopted a new uniform of grey-green tunic and trousers from 1912 onwards. This was essentially the mode of dress for both winter and summer, though there was a winter-issue tunic with a bigger fit to allow the wearing of warm underclothes, and a summer-issue made from a lightweight cotton without breast pockets. The tunic design is very close to that of the Netherlands: single breasted with stand-and-fall collar, and four breast-and side pockets, though there are no shoulder-straps (shoulder-straps were featured on the greatcoat). The rank is displayed on the collar, which also features arm-of-service piping, and also in the lace rows on the slightly archaic kepi. Two badges also grace the kepi: the white, blue and red national cockade, and below it a gilt-metal lion on a red enamelled button.

Date:	April 1940
Unit:	Infantry Division
Rank:	Lieutenant
Theatre:	Arctic
Location:	Norway

Seaman
Armoured Cruiser
Norwegian Navy
Norway 1940

The seaman pictured here is wearing the standard Norwegian Navy uniform which had been issued from 1907. This consists of a blue jumper with a blue-jean collar featuring three white stripes, plus trousers in a matching navy-blue. The jumper was worn with a white shirt underneath and a black scarf around the neck. For ratings, the headgear was a blue hat with a matching pom-pom on top, and the Norwegian cockade centred at the top of the hat with the name of the Royal Norwegian Navy in gold lettering around the headband. Markings on the rest of the uniform are limited to a red fouled anchor with crown, though sometimes this could be sited above one or two red stripes. During summer, navy ratings would be issued with a white version of this uniform, and in winter a thick blue pea-coat was available for protection against cold temperatures.

Date:	April 1940
Unit:	Norwegian Navy
Rank:	Seaman
Theatre:	Baltic
Location:	Norway

Lieutenant No. 331 Squadron Norwegian Air Force England 1941

Though many Norwegians served in the RAF after Norway fell to the Germans in 1940, they were actually granted a separate status from the RAF in 1941. Hence this pilot's uniform is similar to the Royal Air Force in cut, but the Royal Norwegian Air Force had a grey colour of its own, national identification coming from the 'Norway' patch on the left sleeve of the tunic, and the Norway flag on the right (these were also essential in case they were shot down over the UK and local civilians thought they were Germans because of the language difference). Rank, however is British in manner, with this lieutenant having two stars on the tunic collar, while on the matching greatcoat, rank would be up on the shoulder-straps (the greatcoat straps had a silver-lace edging). The peaked cap features the Norwegian cockade surrounded by laurel leaves surmounted by wings.

Date:	September 1941
Unit:	No. 331 Squadron
Rank:	Lieutenant
Theatre:	North-west Europe
Location:	England

Gunner
New Zealand
Artillery
North Africa 1940

The only part of this New Zealand artillery man which would distinguish him from his British allies in the North African theatre would be the distinctive slouch hat, and this also served to prevent NZ troops from being confused with Australian forces. The NZ hat had a pointed crown indented on every quarter with an 'NZ' badge centred and a puggaree with regimental colours worn at the base. The brim of the hat was narrower than the Australian version and was never folded up. Apart from the distinguishing hat, this soldier is wearing standard khaki drill uniforms of British issue, which were given to the NZ force on its arrival in Egypt. The soldier is heavily kitted out in full British 1908-pattern webbing, a webbing system older than the 1937-pattern that most British Army soldiers would have been issued with at this point.

Date:	December 1940
Unit:	New Zealand Artillery
Rank:	Gunner
Theatre:	Mediterranean
Location:	North Africa

Private
ANZ Task Force
South Vietnam
1965

As part of the South-east Asia Treaty Organization (SEATO) Australian and New Zealand both contributed combat troops to the Vietnam conflict; the commitment concluded in 1971. This New Zealander private is seen on a combat patrol wearing standard-issue olive-green fatigues with a matching short-brimmed bush hat. Sensibly, he has covered his webbing straps in waterproof plastic; the Vietnamese jungle climate could easily eat through cloth straps in a matter of weeks. Webbing for NZ troops was usually British or US. His weapon is the FN FAL rifle, the contemporary rifle of the NZ and Australian forces. With its 7.62mm (0.3in) calibre, it was a heavy, long-range weapon, but was also fairly reliable in combat, and so was popular with the troops. The 9mm Sterling SMG was also used.

Date:	1967
Unit:	ANZ Task Force
Rank:	Private
Location:	South Vietnam
Conflict:	Vietnam War

Private
Nigerian
Federal Army
Nigeria 1968

The Nigerian Federal Army has generally been one of the better equipped African armies in the post-war world, though problems of defections and factionalism in the officer class led to it struggling unduly against Biafran independence forces (1967–70). This soldier is seen wearing the green fatigues which, alongside a khaki version, formed the standard uniform of the NFA. These consist of a fairly anonymous shirt and trousers which are worn with British 1958-pattern of webbing with two large ammunition/utility pouches and a water bottle with a 1944-pattern cover. The M1 steel helmet is of US origin. On his feet are British jungle boots, made of rubber and canvas, often seen on the feet of British special forces. His weapon is the venerable and crude Mk II Sten, though NFA soldiers were usually equipped with FN FAL or G3 rifles.

Date:	1968
Unit:	Nigerian Federal Army
Rank:	Private
Location:	Nigeria
Conflict:	Biafran War

Lance-Corporal Pakistani Army Indo-Pakistan Border 1965

The colonial history of Great Britain in the Indian subcontinent is writ large upon the uniform and equipment of this lance-corporal of the Pakistani Army. He wears the standard British Army 1940s and 1950s khaki tropical drill uniform, this being accompanied by British 1937-pattern webbing. It should be noted, however, that Soviet webbing was also worn by the Pakistani and Indian forces. The two large pouches perhaps hold basic rations, personal effects and ammunition, though the rifle slung over his shoulder may be an old Enfield or a civilian weapon. Britain and the US imposed an arms embargo on the region at the outbreak of the Indo-Pakistan conflict, so personal weapons vary greatly in their age and origin. The soldier wears a British steel helmet. The rank chevron's red edging shows his membership of the Frontier Force.

Date:	1965
Unit:	Pakistani Army
Rank:	Lance-Corporal
Location:	Indo-Pakistani Border
Conflict:	Indo-Pakistan War

Private
Pakistani Army
West Pakistan 1971

Even by the 1970s, British equipment and dress were still one of the dominant presences in the military forces of the Indian subcontinent. However, in Pakistan economic constraints meant that this presence was mixed with a whole host of other sources. This soldier is wearing the US M1 steel helmet, but the webbing system is the British Army 1958-pattern. The uniform itself is the Pakistani khaki drill tunic and trousers, this being worn with a V-neck pullover in olive-green which, despite its informal appearance, was a regular item of Pakistani uniform. A piece of equipment which was definitely not of military origin is the canvas shopping bag. The soldier pictured here is using it to carry around some personal effects for which there isn't a proper pouch or backpack. Rank in the Pakistani Army would be displayed on the upper sleeve for the NCOs or on the shoulder-straps for officers.

Date:	1971
Unit:	Pakistani Army
Rank:	Private
Location:	West Pakistan
Conflict:	Indo-Pakistan War

Tank Crewman Armoured Corps Polish Army Poland 1939

This tank crewman would have been lucky to escape with his life during the first months of Germany's Polish campaign. Only 340 inferior Polish tanks faced the onslaught of German mechanized Blitzkrieg, and less than 15 per cent of these survived. This soldier is wearing a uniform with many similarities to French armoured-unit clothing, and the leather crash helmet is actually of French issue. A black beret was often worn under the crash helmet or on its own when outside the vehicle, this matching the black leather coat or long, black greatcoat with which the crews were also issued. Beneath the coat can be seen the two-piece khaki uniform much like that worn by the rest of the Polish Army. On its stand-and-fall collar are the orange-and-black pennants of the armoured corps, while the zigzag embroidery was a feature of officer rank.

Date:	September 1939
Unit:	Armoured Corps
Rank:	Tank Crewman
Theatre:	Eastern Front
Location:	Poland

Captain
Bomber Brigade
Polish Air Force
Poland 1939

This Captain is wearing the Polish Air Force uniform introduced in 1936 as a replacement for the army uniform worn by air-force personnel. Its colour was blue-grey, and consisted of a tunic and matching trousers, with a fall collar for officers and a stand-and-fall collar for other ranks, these being worn with a white shirt and black tie. Rank here is displayed in two locations: on the front of the cap and on the shoulder-straps (the captain's rank is given with three silver stars). The cap depicts the air force version of the Polish national eagle. This eagle motif is repeated in a metal badge on the collar, as worn by all Polish air force staff officers (reserve officer badges featured the letters 'SPR' set within a wreath). On his left breast he wears two badges – including a Pilot Observer badge – and a ceremonial dagger hangs on the left hip.

Date:	September 1939
Unit:	Bomber Brigade
Rank:	Captain
Theatre:	Eastern Front
Location:	Poland

189

Lieutenant Fighter Squadron Polish Air Force Poland 1939

This Polish airman is seen wearing the operational summer uniform. It is a fairly crude outfit consisting of a khaki overall (undyed) made from a stiff linen, this featuring one thigh pocket, one ankle pocket, and two slash pockets on each side at hip level. As the standard blue-grey uniform of the Polish Air Force is obscured, there is little display of rank and insignia. The only marking on the overall is a rank badge on the left sleeve. This was composed of a patch of black cloth, edged in silver thread, with the stars of rank stitched in silver in the centre. For head protection he wears the standard leather flying helmet and goggles, while his neck is warmed by a civilian scarf. A distinct feature of flying officers in the Polish Air Force was wearing a white or gilt metal diving eagle over the left breast pocket, hung from a short length of silver chain.

Date:	September 1939
Unit:	Fighter Squadron
Rank:	Lieutenant
Theatre:	Eastern Front
Location:	Poland

Sergeant
Polish Army in Russia
Russia 1941

The Polish Army in Russia was a unit with a high degree of irony surrounding its formation. It was composed by the Russians at the outbreak of Germany's Operation Barbarossa using Polish POWs which had been captured by Russia during its assault on Poland in 1939. This sergeant is seen here in southern Russia, but was shortly afterwards transferred to service in the Middle East. His uniform is a medley of different items, including British, Russian and Polish kit: the Polish Army in Russia initially wore what it stood in the prison camps, supplemented by private Russian purchases, but was subsequently the recipient of British Army uniforms. Worn here are a khaki drill shirt with cavalry breeches, and puttees, with a British steel helmet (featuring the Polish eagle) and Russian leather webbing. The firearm is the Soviet Tokarev M1940 automatic, a modern weapon for a Polish soldier.

Date:	November 1941
Unit:	Polish Army in Russia
Rank:	Sergeant
Theatre:	Eastern Front
Location:	Southern Russia

Private
II Polish Corps
Italy 1944

The II Polish Corps was formed from Polish soldiers of the Polish Army in Russia who were transferred to Iraq in 1943. Working closely with the British – including accepting most of their uniforms and supplies from the UK – the Poles went on to fight for the Allied cause in Italy, including making a seminal and bloody contribution to the fall of Monte Cassino. This soldier is well-equipped in a mountain-warfare overall, a one-piece thickly padded and waterproof uniform, ideal for snowy mountain conditions. Instead of conventional webbing he wears canvas chest packs with two No.36 British hand-grenades. This uniform and pouches were a British development for commando units operating in arctic/mountainous environments, and would have given excellent protection from northern Italy's climate. Polish soldiers followed British modes of rank display, but the Polish eagle is often seen on their caps and helmets.

Date:	October 1944
Unit:	II Polish Corps
Rank:	Private
Theatre:	Mediterranean
Location:	Italy

Able Seaman
Marynarka Wojenna
Polish Navy
Poland

This naval 'square rig' uniform is of a conventional naval pattern: a naval-blue pullover with a broad, white-striped collar, plus matching trousers with the ankles fixed into white pull-on gaiters. The cap features the Polish eagle and also the name of the ship on which he serves. His tunic has, on his left sleeve, the single gold stripe (edged in red) which, along with a double stripe, indicated the rank of rating, and above it a red badge signifying his speciality: radio technician. Petty officers' badges would be yellow. The Polish Navy uniform varied according to climate. In summer, a white square rig or even British Royal Navy tropical dress would be worn, while officers and petty officers would wear a single-breasted white tunic with a stand collar. This style was maintained in blue for officers and petty officers throughout the rest of the year.

Date:	September 1941
Unit:	*Marynarka Wojenna*
Rank:	Able Seaman
Theatre:	Eastern Front
Location:	Poland

Corporal Portuguese Parachute Regiment Mozambique 1970

The post-war period signalled an intense struggle for Portugal to retain its African possessions, a struggle which lasted well into the 1970s in places such as Guinea-Bissau, Angola and Mozambique. Thus Portugal's armed forces gained a huge wealth of experience in counter-insurgency warfare. This is a corporal of the Portuguese Parachute Regiment, a unit typical of the élite forces usually used in Portugal's colonial conflicts. He wears a 1950 French pattern of camouflage in a distinctive green, brown and olive-green colour scheme. On a practical combat uniform, there is a minimum of insignia. The rank is displayed by the two chevrons on each shoulder slide; membership of the Parachute Regiment is depicted through the para badge on the right breast. The beret badge is that of the Portuguese Air Force.

Date:	1970
Unit:	Portuguese Parachute Regiment
Rank:	Corporal
Location:	Mozambique
Conflict:	Mozambique Independence War

Private
Rhodesian African
Rifles
Rhodesia 1976

The Rhodesian African Rifles proved itself as one of the best counter-insurgency forces in post-war African history. As is expedient given the bush terrain, this soldier is wearing a foliage-pattern of camouflage on his shirt and trousers. He also wears a matching peaked field cap with earflaps, featuring the RAR badge centred on a green-and-black field. The webbing is the British 1958-pattern worn in battle order, with two South African kidney pouches, and the 7.62mm (0.3in) FN MAG was the standard British Army general purpose machine gun. The South African boots have buckled sections which imitate US World War II patterns.

Date:	1976
Unit:	Rhodesian African Rifles
Rank:	Private
Location:	Rhodesian Bush
Conflict:	Rhodesian Civil War

Private Selous Scouts South Rhodesia 1977

Though the Selous Scouts only existed for six years, they have gone down in history as one of the world's best counter-insurgency and reconnaissance units, demonstrating how small, élite units, trained to exceptionally high levels of expertise, could have an effect utterly disproportionate to their size (the entire unit was less than 1500 men). A staggering 68 per cent of nationalist guerrilla fatalities can be laid at the door of the Selous Scouts. On operations, the Scouts travelled extraordinarily light and informally, taking only plenty of water and ammunition. Their 'uniforms' could be nothing more than a pair of shorts and boots. This soldier is dressed more substantially, with a camouflage shirt, woollen hat, British 1958-pattern webbing and hockey boots, also known as 'tackies'. He carries the standard-issue FN FAL rifle.

Date:	1977
Unit:	Selous Scouts
Rank:	Private
Location:	South Rhodesia
Conflict:	Rhodesian Civil War

Guerrilla Fighter Rhodesian Patriotic Front Rhodesia 1979

Though frequently disorganized and under-equipped, the Rhodesian Patriotic Front formed a persistent violent resistance against the white Rhodesian Government. Constructed out of the merging of the Zimbabwe African National Union (ZANU) and the Zimbabwe African People's Union (ZAPU), they were highly motivated for independence. As a guerrilla unit there was no standard uniform, though this soldier is fairly representative. The green beret and T-shirt are civilian, but the trousers are the camouflage combat trousers of the Rhodesian Army. His rifle is the excellent 7.62mm (0.3in) Heckler & Koch G3, and he carries the magazines for this in the series of chest pouches. Ironically, this pattern of load-carrying was used by the RPF's worst opponent, the Selous Scouts; the packs' positioning allows movement through dense foliage.

Date:	1979
Unit:	Rhodesian Patriotic Front
Rank:	Guerrilla Fighter
Location:	Rhodesia/Zimbabwe
Conflict:	Rhodesian Civil War

Rating
Danube Flotilla
Romanian Navy
Black Sea 1941

This rating's uniform has a familiar naval appearance about it. The visible elements are a long, double-breasted greatcoat featuring two rows of gilt metal buttons, blue trousers and ankle boots, and a naval cap with the legend 'Marina Regala' on the band. This cap would also have a ribbon hanging from the back. Beneath the greatcoat, ratings wore a blue jumper with a blue jean collar which had the customary three white stripes, over a blue-and-white striped shirt accompanied by a black scarf (officers wore a similar uniform, though they tended to wear single-breasted blue tunics and peaked caps with black peaks and a yellow metal anchor badge). Rank markings tended to be worn on the upper left sleeve on the tunic – ratings had one to three red stripes – under a speciality badge. Officer rank was sited on the shoulder-straps and collar.

Date:	June 1941
Unit:	Danube Flotilla
Rank:	Rating
Theatre:	Eastern Front
Location:	Black Sea

Lieutenant 2nd *Calarasci* Regiment Russia 1942

This lieutenant is typical of the appearance of a Romanian Army officer in the post-1931 period, the date after which the uniform based itself around British patterns. He wears a single-breasted khaki tunic featuring two breast pockets and two large side pockets, plus in this instance a regimental lanyard running over his left shoulder. Rank is conventionally depicted on the shoulder-straps, while the collar patches denote arm-of-service. The small ribbon beneath his top jacket button is actually that of the German Iron Cross, 2nd Class. Accompanying the tunic is a light khaki shirt and khaki tie and, in this case, cavalry-type pantaloons and riding boots, though more typically the pantaloons would be worn with puttees and ankle boots. The large cap has a Romanian crest, while the cap band is a further indicator of arm-of-service.

Date:	July 1942
Unit:	2nd *Calarasci* Regiment
Rank:	Lieutenant
Theatre:	Eastern Front
Location:	Southern Russia

Private
Infantry Division
Romanian Army
Odessa 1942

Romanian Army uniforms followed a horizon-blue colouration until 1916, from when a khaki pattern was adopted. This soldier is wearing the standard pattern for 1942 on the Eastern Front. The blanket across his chest would give adequate warmth during the summer and autumn months, but this uniform would remain during the Russian winters, when thousands of Romanian soldiers died from frostbite and hypothermia. The basic uniform in summer was a khaki tunic, pantaloons or long trousers (these being worn with puttees or anklets and ankle boots respectively), a lambswool cap, and the Dutch M1928 steel helmet made in Romania under licence. The unpadded greatcoat issued in the winter gave scant protection. The webbing and entrenching tool here are Romanian, whereas the rifle is the German Mauser M1924.

Date:	July 1942
Unit:	Infantry Division
Rank:	Private
Theatre:	Eastern Front
Location:	Odessa

Private
Infantry Division
Romanian Army
Austria 1945

This Romanian soldier shows some of the variations in dress of a field solider from the private seen earlier. He still retains the blanket over his shoulder; in fact, this became a common way of wearing a blanket after Axis troops witnessed Russian forces doing the same on the Eastern Front. His uniform is also the standard khaki combat dress, though here the trousers are worn with knee-high puttees. Instead of the M1928 steel helmet, he wears an unadorned khaki field cap. Other units could have their own dedicated colour schemes; Romanian mountain troops wore a green beret, and armoured personnel a black one. This private carries the Romanian Mannlicher Carbine M1893, a rifle which gave good service in both world wars. He also carries a box of ammunition; note the offset handle which enabled two boxes to be carried in one hand.

Date:	March 1945
Unit:	Infantry Division
Rank:	Private
Theatre:	Eastern Front
Location:	Austria

Private Kimberely Regiment South African Army North Africa 1940

Roughly 140,000 South African troops contributed themselves to the Allied forces in World War II, mainly fighting in the African theatres and also up into Italy. As British Empire forces, their uniforms and kit were in sympathy with that of the British Army. The notable exception here is the sun helmet, chosen in preference to the British steel helmet in Africa, khaki in colour, with a matching puggaree on which featured a cloth patch with regimental or corps colours, and a metal cap badge at the front (this soldier's hat is the 'polo pattern' version). The rest of the uniform consists of a khaki drill jacket with fold-up sleeves, and long trousers worn with the short anklets, these issued from 1940 after Germany declared war on South Africa on 9 September of that year. The .303in Lee Enfield SMLE No.1 Mk III rifle and the 1937-pattern webbing are both British.

Date:	December 1940
Unit:	Kimberley Regiment
Rank:	Private
Theatre:	Mediterranean
Location:	North Africa

Lieutenant
Royal South African
Air Force
North Africa 1942

South Africa fielded a small but competent air force which had a significant impact in some African theatres, particularly in Abyssinia, where it destroyed around 95 Italian aircraft. South Africa also provided the RAF with some of its most notable aces, including 'Sailor' Malan who accounted for some 27 aircraft during the Battle of Britain. The flying officer here looks in most regards like an army soldier. This was due to the air force actually being formed under the auspices of the army in 1920, and thus army uniforms were adopted. The difference from the army lies purely in the insignia: air force wings on the left breast, with an air force badge surmounting the sun helmet and a blue arm-of-service patch on the puggaree. The orange-red flash on the shoulder-straps are a further air force indicator, these sharing the straps with the officer's rank.

Date:	October 1942
Unit:	Royal South African Air Force
Rank:	Lieutenant
Theatre:	Mediterranean
Location:	North Africa

203

Private
South African Army
Namibia 1980

South Africa fought a long and bitter counter-insurgency conflict within Namibia from the late 1960s to 1988, the date on which Namibia achieved full independence from South Africa, even though it had been granted this in theory by the UN in 1966. Combat against the South West African People's Organization (SWAPO), mainly based in Angola, was a hot affair, so uniforms tended towards simplicity and light materials. This soldier wears a cotton two-piece khaki uniform, the shirt and trousers having the additional feature of covered pocket buttons to stop the buttons snagging on foliage when on patrol. His webbing system priorities are food and water. Around the back would be a water bottle centred on the belt and flanked by two kidney pouches for rations, survival gear and personal effects. To the front are two large ammunition pouches, each holding two magazines for his FN FAL rifle.

Date:	1980
Unit:	South African Army
Rank:	Private
Theatre:	Namibia
Location:	Namibian Independence War

Sergeant
SA Recon Commando
South African Bush
1990s

The South African Recon Commandos are South Africa's counter-insurgency élite, specializing in deep-penetration into the African bush as well as urban combat and specialist parachute techniques. Only about 8 per cent of people who begin Recon training pass the course. Here a heavily armed 'Recce' is on a patrol, his uniform the standard khaki shirt, trousers and slouch hat worn by all South African soldiers. However, Recces are also seen in several foliage-pattern camouflages, including varieties which mix vivid blues and mustards. His load-carrying equipment is South African; the Recces had a double-sided rucksack made for them which sat a parachute in the middle so that packs could be standardized across airborne and ground operations. His rifle, the Israeli 5.56mm (0.22in) Galil, is supplemented by two IMI rifle-grenades.

Date:	1990s
Unit:	Reconnaissance Commandos
Rank:	Sergeant
Location:	South African Bush
Conflict:	None

Infantryman Spanish Blue Division Ukraine 1942

Though Franco's Spain was essentially pro-Axis during World War II, the catastrophe of the Spanish Civil War ensured that it would remain neutral throughout the conflict. However, the Spanish Blue Division – later the 250th Infantry Division – of some 18,000 volunteers was sent to Germany's aid on the Eastern Front. Deployed to Russia in July 1941, it suffered 60 per cent casualties in the fighting, and the survivors came home in October 1943. Here we see a Spanish infantryman in standard German field-grey infantry uniform and kit, including an MP40 submachine gun. A badge on the right sleeve displays the national colours on a shield patch, this also being repeated up on the helmet. The name 'Blue Division' came from the Falangist Party (Spanish fascist) blue shirts, worn under the German uniforms.

Date:	June 1942
Unit:	Spanish Blue Division
Rank:	Infantryman
Theatre:	Eastern Front
Location:	Ukraine

Legionnaire
Spanish
Foreign Legion
Canary Islands 1987

The Spanish Foreign Legion is a national unit which does not accept foreigners. It is a crack force with a training and discipline similar to the French Foreign Legion. Soldiers wear the grey shirt and trousers of the regular Spanish Army, though with distinguishing features unique to the unit. The first of these is the black boots with three buckles down the side. The second is the side cap with red tassel. However, soldiers also wear a green beret registered to the left. This soldier wears the Spanish Army fatigues, but Legion soldiers also wear camouflage when necessary, with modern steel- or ballistic nylon helmets. He carries the 7.62mm (0.3in) CETME rifle, whose calibre became 5.56mm (0.22in) NATO standard in the 1980s.

Date:	1987
Unit:	Spanish Foreign Legion
Rank:	Legionnaire
Location:	Canary Islands
Conflict:	None

Officer
Spanish GEO
Madrid 1990s

The *Grupo Especial de Operaciones* (GEO) was formed in the 1970s as Spain's answer to an increase in terrorism within its borders and external interests, particularly from the Basque-separatist organization, ETA, in the north. Its members are trained in surveillance, hostage-rescue and VIP protection. The officer here cannot be said to wear typical GEO dress, as the unit selects weaponry and equipment to suit each individual role. However, the Spanish-made leaf-pattern camouflage is commonly used. Here, it is imposed on a one-piece combat overall with minimal insignia, but a unit badge on the right sleeve. This probably indicates that this officer is on training, when insignia is left off for security purposes, while the balaclava obscures his features. He carries a Heckler & Koch MP5A2, and a H & K 9mm P-9S automatic on his belt.

Date:	1990s
Unit:	GEO
Rank:	Counter-Terrorist Officer
Location:	Madrid
Conflict:	None

Private
Syrian Army
Golan Heights 1973

Revitalized by greater investment in training and rearmament with modern Soviet weapons, in 1973 the Syrian Army launched a powerful assault upon Israeli positions on the Golan Heights as part of the Arab onslaught known as the Yom Kippur War. However, the Israeli positions were too entrenched and the Syrians inadvisably relied on armour in the mountainous terrain and were again defeated. This private on the Golan Heights is dressed in uniform and equipment which is almost entirely of Soviet- or communist-Europe issue. He holds an AK-47 assault rifle, which is an excellent close-quarters weapon. Indeed, it had such an impact during the Yom Kippur War that it forced the Israelis to redevelop and improve their own small arms. The private's camouflage shirt and trousers are of East German origin, although they have a French style of camouflage, and the helmet is the standard issue Soviet infantry headgear.

Date:	1973
Unit:	Syrian Army
Rank:	Private
Location:	Golan Heights
Conflict:	Yom Kippur War

Corporal
Syrian Army
Beirut 1982

The city of Beirut was a hideous cauldron for many forces in the early 1980s, not least the Syrian Army. Having suffered terrible losses in Israel's 1982 'Peace for Galilee' invasion of the Lebanon, large elements of the Syrian forces then had to face vicious inter-faction warfare within the confines of Lebanon itself. This soldier's green beret indicates that he is probably a special forces soldier, though many units' dress became somewhat unorthodox during the conflict in Beirut. His uniform is plain olive-drab trousers and shirt in a Soviet pattern (Syrian commandos could also be seen in a 'lizard-pattern' camouflage). As these items are fairly commonplace, it is the webbing that captures the attention: Communist in origin, it shows the Chinese practice of placing AK magazines in curved pouches on the chest.

Date:	1982
Unit:	Syrian Army
Rank:	Corporal
Location:	Beirut
Conflict:	Israeli invasion of Lebanon

Private
Turkish Army
Gallipoli 1916

The Turkish defence of Gallipoli is seen historically as one of the great Turkish victories of World War I. In this action, the Turkish Army repelled the Allied invasion force, even though it suffered the loss of hundreds of thousands of its soldiers. This private here is seen at Gallipoli wearing the standard olive-drab uniform of the Turkish Army. The shirt, trousers, puttees and shoes are all internationally conventional: the headgear is not. For headgear, Turkish soldiers wore either the traditional fez or the cloth-covered solar topi, as shown here. The absence of brim on both of these items was intentional, as it followed the Islamic belief that it is wrong to shield your eyes from the sun. Over his tunic this soldier wears a cartridge belt, and the rounds are exposed under the leather flaps of the pouches. He carries the 7.65mm (0.301in) Rifle M1890, a Turkish version of the German Mauser.

Date:	1916
Unit:	Turkish Army
Rank:	Private
Theatre:	Southern Europe
Location:	Gallipoli

Private Turkish Army Cyprus 1974

This Turkish soldier involved in the invasion of Cyprus in 1974 illustrates some of the anomalies in uniform and kit that were common in the Turkish forces at the time. His shirt and trousers are simple olive-drab fatigues of Turkish origin, probably made in cotton, these being worn with a matching beret (DPM camouflage was not introduced until the 1980s in Turkey). His helmet, however, is the US M1 carrying the camouflage scheme used by US Marines and other units during the Pacific campaign of World War II. In keeping with the World War II theme, he also carries a .45in M3 submachine gun, a crude weapon even in the days of World War II but positively archaic by the 1970s (production finished in 1944). The webbing straps belong to the US M1943 pattern, though here they are fitted with Turkish ammunition pouches which are too short to take the M3's magazines.

Date:	1974
Unit:	Turkish Army
Rank:	Private
Location:	Cyprus
Conflict:	Turkish Invasion of Cyprus

Sergeant British Royal Horse Artillery France 1914

As war broke out in 1914, the British Army was tasked with finding uniforms not only for its regular soldiers, but also for millions of conscripts. Thus it was common for soldiers in the first years of the war to be wearing older patterns of clothing and equipment. This sergeant is wearing the standard British Army uniform in the tunic, trousers and puttees, the peaked service cap also being standard dress until an unacceptably high percentage of head casualties on the Western Front led to the introduction of the Mk 1 steel helmet in 1916. On this cap is the standard cap badge of the Royal Regiment of Artillery, a cannon surmounted by a crown, and the motto 'Ubique' (Everywhere). The ammunition bandolier is the outdated 1903-pattern, with 50 rounds for a Lee Enfield rifle, replaced in 1908 by a superior load-carrying system.

Date:	1914
Unit:	British Royal Horse Artillery
Rank:	Sergeant
Theatre:	Western Front
Location:	France

Private Royal Marines Antwerp 1914

Antwerp was the first operational destination for the Royal Marines in World War I. A Royal Marine brigade was formed in August 1914 and then deployed at very short notice to Antwerp in a futile attempt to stop German capture of this vital port. Such was the speed of their deployment that many soldiers arrived at Ostend prior to the mission in their full-dress uniforms – combat outfits had not been issued. However, this soldier presents a typical view of an RM soldier in 1914. He is wearing the standard British Army khaki serge uniform instead of the blue uniform worn by pre-war RM units. His web gaiters, however, are actually Royal Navy issue. The only designations of his RM status are the 'RMLI' (Royal Marine Light Infantry) badges set on the shoulder straps and the RM badge centred on the field cap. His webbing is the 1908 pattern, featuring multiple ammunition pouches for his .303in (7.7mm) SMLE rifle.

Date:	October 1914
Unit:	Royal Marine Light Infantry
Rank:	Private
Theatre:	Western Front
Location:	Antwerp

Lieutenant Royal Navy Jutland 1916

The uniform of the Royal Navy settled into an established pattern in the nineteenth century, and it was this pattern (with minor variations) which took naval officers and rating through the two world wars of the twentieth century. Here we see a lieutenant wearing a mix of his naval whites and his standard service jacket and cap. The jacket was a double-breasted 'reefer' type. It had two rows of gold buttons running down the front, while rank was kept simply to gold lace around the cuffs, the upper row always featuring a loop. This jacket was generally worn with a white shirt and black tie, though here this officer wears a white cravat to protect against the cold of the North Sea. His cap is peaked, with a mohair band 44.5mm (1.75in) deep and the Royal Navy badge consisting of a silver anchor and royal crown surrounded by gold laurel leaves. The battle of Jutland was an indecisive affair, both sides claiming victory.

Date:	1916
Unit:	Royal Navy
Rank:	Lieutenant
Theatre:	Northern Europe
Location:	North Sea

Private British Army Cambrai 1916

This British Army private offers a representative view of the British soldier who fought in the trenches of the Western Front. The UK military introduced a khaki service dress for personnel in India in 1885, but in 1902 khaki became the standard colour of military battledress throughout the British Army (it should be noted that some soldiers arrived in France in blue serge outfits because of uniform shortages; these outfits were later used to clothe British POWs in Germany). The Mk 1 steel helmet formed the basic headgear (introduced in 1916), while all ranks wore a khaki tunic with four patch pockets, matching trousers, puttees wound up to the knee, and black boots or shoes. Equipment is carried with the 1908-pattern webbing, an '08 gas-mask pack at the ready on this soldier's chest, and the rifle he carries on his left side is the .303in (7.7mm) Lee-Enfield Mk III SMLE.

Date:	1916
Unit:	British Army
Rank:	Private
Theatre:	Western Front
Location:	Cambrai

2nd Lieutenant Artist's Rifles France 1916

This lieutenant of the Artist's Rifles gives an especially clear view of the 1908-pattern webbing worn by almost all British soldiers during World War I. Though he is actually wearing the officer's version (by virtue of the Webley revolver in the holster on his hip), most of the other items are in their standard infantry configuration. The 1908-pattern webbing was designed to replace and expand the 1903 Bandolier Equipment, which had no knapsack or pack and featured a bandolier and a waistbelt with a total of 10 ammunition pouches each holding 10 rounds. Tests in 1906 and 1907 produced an alternative 10 sets of webbing, which distilled into the 1908-pattern in January of that year. The new webbing consisted of a waistbelt and braces, 10 ammunition pockets holding 15 rounds each, bayonet frog, water-bottle carrier, haversack and pack, entrenching-tool carrier for haft (seen here) and head.

Date:	1916
Unit:	Artist's Rifles
Rank:	2nd Lieutenant
Theatre:	Western Front
Location:	France

Captain
Royal Flying Corps
France 1917

Shy and introspective, Captain Albert Ball nevertheless became one of Britain's greatest (and most reluctant) war heroes. In total he was responsible for downing 44 German aircraft, and he went on to receive the Victoria Cross for his efforts. Here we see him in a typical pose for the British newspapers, holding the propeller and spinner of his Nieuport 17 Scout aircraft. However, it was on 7 May 1917, while flying a British SE.5 aircraft – which he disliked – that he met his fate, and was killed in a dogfight in stormy weather. Officers of the Royal Flying Corps generally wore the uniforms of the regiments to which they had originally been attached. Thus Captain Ball is seen here wearing standard British Army field dress with service cap, with the Royal Flying Corps badge in its customary position, on the left of the cap. Rank is displayed on the cuffs, and the collar features the Royal Flying Corps badge.

Date:	1917
Unit:	Royal Flying Corps
Rank:	Captain
Theatre:	Western Front
Location:	France

Pilot
Royal Flying Corps
France 1917

Royal Flying Corps pilots on the ground wore either standard British Army service dress with Royal Flying Corps insignia or the 1903-pattern dress with a lancer-type jacket which was commonly known as the 'maternity jacket'. However, once airborne, it was necessary to wear clothing that would protect the pilot from the biting winds of an open cockpit at high altitudes. Here we see a downed British pilot wearing typical Royal Flying Corps flying gear. A long leather coat and silk scarf provide the main elements of the outfit, while fur-lined boots and flying helmet shielded the feet and the head respectively. Long gauntlet-type gloves would also be fur-lined for warmth. The pilot shown here is making a defiant gesture to his adversary by shooting off a few rounds from his Webley Mk IV revolver; Webley revolvers were the standard side-arm of RFC pilots throughout the war.

Date:	1917
Unit:	Royal Flying Corps
Rank:	Pilot
Theatre:	Western Front
Location:	France

Lieutenant Tank Corps France 1918

This soldier of the Tank Corps is, on the whole, wearing the standard British Army service dress, though with some notable variations. Most conspicuous of these is the chain-mail face mask. This was designed to protect the face from steel splinters caused by enemy small-arms fire, as the armour of the early British tanks could be quite insubstantial. Shorts are also worn instead of the issue trousers. These were advisable items of clothing inside the tanks, which had notoriously bad ventilation and, in combat, produced internal temperatures which made many a crew pass out through heat exhaustion. A respirator is carried in a bag over the right shoulder, as much to save the crewman from internal fumes as from the dangers of an enemy gas attack. By 1918 the Tank Corps had been armed with Mk A Medium Tanks ('Whippet') which could travel at a top speed of 12.8km/h (8mph).

Date:	1918
Unit:	Tank Corps
Rank:	Private
Theatre:	Western Front
Location:	France

Airman
Bomber Command
Royal Air Force
England 1939

The early years of World War II were a testing time for RAF Bomber Command, as both its light- and heavy bombers were intensely vulnerable to German fighter superiority. However, with the later introduction of the Avro Lancaster, strategic bombing began to make an impact, particularly in Germany's industrial heartland and in support of Allied D-Day landings. Bombing raids were freezing, uncomfortable experiences for the crew; this pilot wears a thermally insulated jacket made from glazed sheepskin by the Irvin Parachute Co. (whose parachute harness he wears). The leggings have large patch pockets for mapwork. Boots and helmet are thickly padded. A welcome innovation was electrically heated gloves and boots, supplied with power by a cable that ran down through the jacket sleeves and legs.

Date:	September 1939
Unit:	Bomber Command
Rank:	Airman
Theatre:	North-west Europe
Location:	England

Private
The East Yorkshire
Regiment
Maginot Line 1940

This soldier presents a uniform which was not typically seen on British soldiers in World War II. Over his khaki service dress he wears a large snowsuit made from padded material. The jacket is double-breasted to provide better wind resistance, while the Mk 1 steel helmet is covered in a white snow-cover for additional camouflage. Snowsuits were not a large-scale standard-issue item of clothing for the British forces during the war, and this suit was issued to this soldier especially for his chilly guard duty at the French Maginot Line in the deep winter of 1940. Over the front of his uniform he wears a cotton ammunition bandolier, issued as part of the 1937-pattern webbing. The bandolier had five pockets, each of these holding two five-round clips of .303in (7.7mm) ammunition for the Lee Enfield No.1 Mk III rifle, seen here.

Date:	January 1940
Unit:	The East Yorkshire Regiment
Rank:	Private
Theatre:	North-west Europe
Location:	Maginot Line

Captain Home Fleet Royal Navy Great Britain 1940

This Captain of the Home Fleet illustrates perfectly the standard uniform worn by Royal Navy officers during World War II. Working from the top down, we have a blue, navy cloth peaked cap with a black mohair band and a black, patent calf-leather peak and chin-strap. The badge in the centre of the cap has a silver anchor at its centre, surrounded by gold laurel leaves and surmounted by a gold-and-silver crown on a red backing. As a senior officer, this captain also has gold leaves on the peak, stitched onto a blue cloth peak-cover. The rest of the uniform consists of a double-breasted 'reefer' jacket with double-row gold buttons, worn with a white shirt and black tie, blue trousers and black shoes. In addition to the leaves on his cap peak, his rank is indicated by the gold rings around the sleeve. The purple rings between these refer to the arm-of-service.

Date:	January 1940
Unit:	Home Fleet
Rank:	Captain
Theatre:	North-west Europe
Location:	Great Britain

Private 49th Infantry Division Narvik 1940

Because of his long, voluminous coat, this soldier can at first be confused with a naval rating, though he is actually a private of the 49th Infantry Division seen during the Norwegian campaign of 1940. The coat was termed the 'tropal' coat and was lined with kapok, a cotton-like substance used to pad clothes and also to stuff items like cushions. This padding made the coat very warm, but it also made it bulky and inhibiting to movement. It was fastened with metal clips and had two deep, flapped pockets. Beneath the coat, the soldier is wearing standard khaki service dress, and anklets are visible. The webbing is the 1937-pattern. The pouches at either side are ammunition pouches which were designed to take either two Bren gun magazines (he holds one in his hand) or cotton bandoliers of Lee Enfield ammunition. In the centre is the 1937 haversack, turned around and worn as a pack, a common technique.

Date:	April 1940
Unit:	49th Infantry Division
Rank:	Private
Theatre:	Arctic
Location:	Narvik

Lance-Corporal 4th Infantry Division France 1940

We see here a lance-corporal of the Scottish Black Watch Regiment, a regiment which, like most north of the Scottish border, adapted standard British Army dress to give it a local and national flavour. Instead of the standard British Army khaki-serge tunic, he wears a cutaway version known as a doublet, the matching khaki trousers being omitted in favour of a regimental kilt. In addition, the Mk 1 steel helmet is replaced with a 'Tam o'shanter' beret featuring a khaki pom-pom on top and a red regimental hackle at the side, though in combat the steel helmet would naturally make a reappearance. The tunic is heavily decorated with various badges and insignia. The single chevron denotes rank, while the circular red badge is a formation sign of the 4th Division. The crossed rifles indicate marksmanship proficiency, and the wheel above is a driver's qualification.

Date:	May 1940
Unit:	4th Infantry Division
Rank:	Lance-Corporal
Theatre:	North-west Europe
Location:	France

Sergeant
11 Group
Royal Air Force
Home Counties 1940

This sergeant's steel helmet alludes to the likelihood of Luftwaffe attack against British airfields during 1940, as usually the RAF personnel wore a field service cap or, for officers, the peaked cap with a metal badge. The rest of the uniform is similar in cut to the British Army service dress, except that it is rendered in the Royal Air Force blue. It is made from serge, and featured a single-breasted tunic with two breast- and two side patch pockets, long, blue trousers and black shoes. The tunic was worn over a white shirt and black tie. Rank was given in the conventional pattern – here three chevrons on each sleeve in worsted on a black background – though if wearing overalls or shirt sleeves, armlets would often be used. This sergeant also carries a Webley pistol in a holster, the ammunition being carried in the pouch on the right hip.

Date:	July 1940
Unit:	11 Group
Rank:	Sergeant
Location:	North-west Europe
Conflict:	Home Counties

Sergeant
Welsh Guards
Household Division
England 1940

By 1940 a new battledress for British Army soldiers had been established. Introduced in 1937, this consisted of khaki blouse and long trousers, both roomy in the cut, with the trousers gathered at the ankle and fitted into the boots. This sergeant's khaki service dress pre-dates this uniform, and harks back to the World War I British Army uniform, elements of which were still worn in the early years of World War II. The most anachronistic items are the long puttees wrapped around the calves and the leather jerkin overcoat lined with khaki material. His webbing, however, is up-to-date; the 1937-pattern in olive-drab with a backpack and two large ammunition pouches fastened to the front of the belt (he also carries a khaki pack for personal effects). He carries the standard rifle of the British Army in 1940: the .303in (7.7mm) No. 1 SMLE.

Date:	September 1940
Unit:	Welsh Guards
Rank:	Sergeant
Theatre:	North-west Europe
Location:	Pirbright

Corporal 6th Royal Tank Regiment North Africa 1941

Generally, British Army tank crews wore standard British Army uniforms with insignia and headgear variations. There was more variation in the northern theatres, where tank crews were seen wearing a black denim overall over their service dress, but even this became consigned to training crews as the war progressed. For the North African theatre, lightness of dress was essential, and so tank crews took the army khaki shirt and shorts, here worn with woollen socks, puttees and ankle boots. The tunic bears the rank on the right sleeve, while the shoulder-straps display the colours of the 6th Tank Regiment. He also has a regimental lanyard running under the left shoulder. The hat is the black beret of the Royal Tank Regiment, complete with silver regimental cap badge. Inside the tank, a black fibre helmet would probably be worn.

Date:	January 1941
Unit:	6th Royal Tank Regiment
Rank:	Sergeant
Theatre:	Mediterranean
Location:	North Africa

Rating
HMS *Warspite*
Royal Navy
Crete 1941

Being a gun crewmember was one of the most physically demanding tasks aboard a warship, as is suggested by the size of this shell for one of *Warspite*'s eight 6in (152mm) guns (*Warspite* also had 8 15in (381mm) and 8 4in (102mm) guns). This rating is seen during the ferocious naval battles which took place off Crete, the site of possibly the worst Royal Navy action of the war, with over 2000 men lost and 18 warships sunk or badly damaged. The uniform is designed to be hard-wearing and protective. Over his naval dress he has a heavy toggle-fastened duffel coat and life-jacket. His trousers are bell-bottomed and tucked into rubber boots with heavy socks. Under his standard British steel helmet he also wears an asbestos anti-flash hood designed to protect the wearer during firing and also from the flash ignition of the cordite propellants.

Date:	March 1941
Unit:	HMS *Warspite*
Rank:	Rating
Theatre:	Mediterranean
Location:	Off Crete

Captain 3rd King's Own Hussars North Africa 1941

Apart from the cap, this cavalry officer wears the standard tropical version of the khaki service dress (though officers usually had a uniform of better tailoring than lower ranks). This was a lightweight uniform made from gabardine, barathea or khaki drill, seen here as a shirt and long trousers, though a tunic and shorts were also part of the dress. The rubber-soled suede 'chukka' boots were actually not official issue (the service dress uniform came with khaki field boots or shoes), but they were popular amongst officers for their comfort in desert conditions. Webbing is the officer's version of the 1937-pattern, this having a holster for a Webley pistol (here seen with a pouch for ammunition), while on the opposite hip is a compass holder. The distinct cavalry item is the bright-red cap, with the badge of the 3rd King's Own Hussars offset to the left.

Date:	October 1941
Unit:	3rd King's Own Hussars
Rank:	Captain
Theatre:	Mediterranean
Location:	North Africa

Pilot
No. 112 Squadron
Royal Air Force
North Africa 1941

During World War II, No. 112 Squadron undertook operations in more theatres than many RAF units, first in North Africa, then in Italy and Sicily, finally coming to the northern European theatre for the Allied D-Day landings and beyond. They flew primarily in ground-attack roles, first in the outdated Gloster Gladiator biplanes, but progressing to Curtiss Tomahawks then P-51 Mustangs. This pilot here is seen in North Africa in late 1941, wearing a lightweight khaki overall issued to pilots in tropical zones. His headgear is the leather flying helmet Type B, which was able to accept external communications wires. Slung low behind his knees is his Irvin parachute. The harness features a quick-release mechanism to release all harness straps with a single turn. The actual parachute release handle is sited just under the left forearm.

Date:	November 1941
Unit:	No. 112 Squadron
Rank:	Pilot
Theatre:	Mediterranean
Location:	North Africa

Sergeant
No.1 Commando
HMS *Campbeltown*
St Nazaire 1942

An early morale-lifter for the British during World War II was the Royal Navy and Commando raid on the German dry dock at St Nazaire in March 1942. Though nearly 400 soldiers did not come home, including 197 killed, the raid destroyed the dock and severely prohibited Germany's use of capital ships in Atlantic operations. A commando solider is seen here checking two magazines for a Sten submachine gun. He wears a khaki battledress, the trousers being fastened into light khaki anklets and over the top of the boots. These commonly worn boots, with thickly treaded rubber soles, were known as 'ammunition' boots. As a member of the demolition part of the raid, he has plentiful hand-grenades in his front pouches and a Browning automatic pistol. A definitive commando item is the Fairburn-Sykes combat knife in a dedicated slot in the trousers.

Date:	28 March 1942
Unit:	No. 1 Commando
Rank:	Sergeant
Theatre:	North-west Europe
Location:	St Nazaire

Wing Commander No. 617 Squadron Royal Air Force England 1943

Pictured here is the infamous Wing Commander Guy Gibson, leader of the 'Dambuster' No. 617 squadron. His uncompromising and skilled leadership led to the smashing of the Ruhr dams and his award of the Victoria Cross. His uniform is the standard blue-grey battledress issued to RAF personnel, with additions for operational status. Over the uniform he wears the yellow Type LS inflatable life-jacket, while clutched in his right hand is the Type C leather flying helmet. His headgear in this case is his officer's service cap, with a black band and the RAF eagle and badge. Rank is displayed on the shoulder-straps. One item of interest is his fleece-lined flying boots, which provided good heat retention for the pilot, even at high altitudes. However, if he was shot down, he could cut away the top of the boots and leave a functional pair of ground boots.

Date:	May 1943
Unit:	No. 617 Squadron
Rank:	Wing Commander
Theatre:	North-west Europe
Location:	England

233

Admiral
Mediterranean Fleet
Royal Navy
Egypt 1943

He we see Admiral Sir John Cunningham, the Naval Commander-in-Chief Levant, wearing the regulation Royal Navy whites worn by officers on ceremonial or tropical operational duties. The cap could be made with a white top, but an equal option was to fit a white, washable cover over the standard naval blue cap. His rank is indicated by the leaves embroidered along the cap-peak and also on the shoulder-straps: a crown, crossed sword and three eight-pointed stars. Arm-of-service was indicated by the border of the shoulder-straps, most professions displaying a blue border. Ceremonial features of Cunningham's dress include the M1891 naval officer's sword, while the three medals on his tunic are the Order of Bath (top), the Norwegian Royal Order of St Olaf, and the Royal Greek Order of George I.

Date:	September 1943
Unit:	Mediterranean Fleet
Rank:	Admiral
Theatre:	Mediterranean
Location:	Cairo

Lieutenant
1st Glider
Pilot Regiment
Normandy 1944

This soldier – Lieutenant J.F. Hubble of the 1st Glider Pilot Regiment – is here seen just after the airlanding of British troops which was undertaken as part of the initial waves of the D-Day invasion force. The treacherous nature of glider landings is suggested by the fibre crash-helmet worn over the Type C flying helmet, while a Type F oxygen mask speaks of the lack of pressurization in the basic Horsa gliders. Though a pilot, Lt Hubble's uniform shows his allegiance to the airborne forces of the British Army. His camouflage overcoat is the paratrooper's Denison smock, while in his right hand he holds the paras' red beret. To signify that he is a glider pilot, he wears glider wings over his left breast. Glider pilots who weren't members of the army also wore white parachutes or gliders embroidered on the left sleeve in a pale-blue thread.

Date:	6 June 1944
Unit:	1st Glider Pilot Regiment
Rank:	Lieutenant
Theatre:	North-west Europe
Location:	Normandy

Head Officer Royal Observer Corps, RAF England 1944

Though in military dress, this officer is actually part of the civilian Observer Corps. The Observer Corps was established in 1918, fell under the jurisdiction of the Royal Air Force in 1929, and became known as the Royal Observer Corps after the award of a royal warrant in 1941. It was during this year that the Corps finally moved from civilian- to military dress. This new uniform was the RAF grey-serge battledress. The tunic featured the badge of the ROC surmounted by a crown, this badge being repeated up on the cap (the badge featured an Elizabethan coastal watcher and the motto 'Forewarned is Forearmed'). The cap was black, though a black steel helmet was also worn. This officer has a 'Head Observer' panel over his left breast while the Spitfire badge sewn on the sleeve indicates his status as a 'Master Spotter'.

Date:	June 1944
Unit:	Royal Observer Corps
Rank:	Head Officer
Theatre:	North-west Europe
Location:	Kent

Groundcrew Fire-Fighting Unit Royal Air Force Malaya 1945

Fire-fighting was a tremendously dangerous job for RAF personnel, as airfields and aircraft usually have copious amounts of ammunition, aviation fuel, kerosene and other flammable substances present. This groundcrew wears the full protective suit designed for tackling chronic fires, made from asbestos and with full-body coverage and the minimum of joints that might be wrenched open by blast. The asbestos jacket is double-breasted and secured with a metal clasp and a chain. The trousers cover the entire foot and are rubber soled at the bottom. Elbow-length gloves give substantial protection to the hands. Headgear is a large hood zipped into place, and vision is provided through a tinted and reinforced glass plate at the front. This fire-fighting clothing was issued to RAF units at home and abroad.

Date:	June 1945
Unit:	South-east Asia Command
Rank:	Private
Theatre:	Pacific
Location:	Malaya

Marine
Royal Marines
Chosin 1950

Though this soldier is a Royal Marine Commando, his uniform and kit are US supplied, issued to the Marines in Japan prior to their deployment to the Korean conflict. The M1943 combat dress was a seminal advance in post-war uniform design, working on a modern layered principle which recognized the fact that many thinner layers of clothing give the wearer more control over warmth than few thick layers. Visible here are the top layers (khaki battledress is worn underneath), a windproof and waterproof jacket and trousers of heavy-duty cotton sateen material. Over the jacket is the US M1943 web belt. This features four ammunition pouches for his M1 Garand rifle, and a small medical pouch which hangs beneath the belt from cords on the right hip (a penknife also hangs from the belt). The M1943 formed the basis of future British uniform design, leading to the 1950-pattern combat dress.

Date:	1950
Unit:	Royal Marines
Rank:	Marine
Location:	Chosin
Conflict:	Korean War

Corporal Gloucestershire Regiment South Korea 1951

This soldier is kitted out in the British 1950-pattern battledress, based on the US M1943 layered uniform system which proved reasonably successful in coping with the full climate range of Korea. Here the soldier is wearing the basic serge shirt and trousers, though there was also a weather-proof smock which could be worn as an outer layer. Further environmental protection came with the issue of a special parka coat and sleeping bag which, along with the large-toed boots, became the British Army's 'Cold/Wet Weather' uniform for Korean service. The cap, however, is US Army arctic-environment issue. Markings are minimal: just two chevrons denoting the rank on the sleeve, while the Gloucestershire's name is worn on the upper sleeve above the circular badge indicating the 29th British Independent Infantry Brigade.

Date:	1951
Unit:	Gloucestershire Regiment
Rank:	Corporal
Theatre:	South Korea
Location:	Korean War

Marine
Royal Marines
Malaya 1952

Between 1948 and 1960 the British Army was locked in a substantial counter-insurgency war with the Communist Malayan Races Liberation Army (MRLA), a guerrilla movement fighting for independence. British troops developed their jungle combat tactics to a fine degree in Malaya, so much so that US special forces utilized their tactical manuals during the Vietnam conflict. This Marine wears a combination of items ideally suited for manoeuvres in the hot and humid South-east Asian jungles. An olive-drab fatigue shirt is worn with Marine-issue trousers, these being tucked tightly into boots to stop the trousers snagging on foliage and also to keep out insects. The boots are canvas and leather, hardier than all-leather boots. Equipment is held in 1944-pattern webbing, and the weapon is the exceptionally durable Australian 9mm Owen submachine gun. The white marking on his cap acts as a unit identifier on patrols.

Date:	1952
Unit:	Royal Marines
Rank:	Marine
Location:	Malaya
Conflict:	Malayan Emergency

Private
3rd Battalion
Parachute Regiment
Suez 1956

When in operational clothing, from 1941 British paras often wore the Denison smock, consisting of a thigh-length waterproof and windproof jacket. It came in a camouflage mix of olive-green, ochre and yellows. On the sleeve of his smock this para wears the regiment's wings in white on a khaki field. Beneath that a green flash signifies his drop zone and membership of 3 Para. He wears 1950-pattern khaki battledress and a sand-coloured helmet, and commando-type boots with thick, heavily treaded rubber soles. Like most paras on operations, he carries large amounts of kit in the 1944-pattern webbing system: a backpack and bedding roll, an oilskin for wrapping weapons in, a water bottle, a first-aid pack, and ammunition pouches at the front.

Date:	1956
Unit:	3rd Bn, Parachute Regiment
Rank:	Private
Location:	Gamil Airfield
Conflict:	Suez Invasion

Trooper 22 SAS Regiment Oman 1959

This soldier is seen here at the Jebel Akhdar, a mountainous plateau in Oman which was the stronghold for anti-government rebels in Oman's civil war. This war erupted in 1957 and the SAS was brought in at the request of Sultan Said bin Taimur for assistance in counter-insurgency. As the attack against Jebel Akhdar began at night, this trooper's uniform is designed around warmth rather than protection from the daytime heat of Oman's deserts. His jacket is the British paratrooper's standard Denison smock, zipper-fastened at the collar and camouflaged in natural foliage shades, and providing a good measure of protection against the wind-chill factor. He wears standard British Army battledress trousers and gaiters, and the 1944-pattern web belt. The hobnailed leather boots proved a genuine problem: the Jebel Akhdar is mostly metallic rock, where the boots split apart or slipped.

Date:	1959
Unit:	22 SAS Regiment
Rank:	Trooper
Location:	Jebel Akhdar, Oman
Conflict:	Omani Civil War

Rifleman
7th Gurkha Rifles
Borneo 1966

This Gurkha soldier is carrying the US M16A1 rifle on this jungle patrol in 1966, instead of the standard British Army rifle, the L1A1 SLR. The Gurkhas chose the lighter and shorter M16 because their smaller frames could better handle it; it also had considerably less recoil than the SLR. Otherwise he is dressed and equipped in the standard British Army tropical combat dress: a plain olive-drab shirt and trousers, and matching slouch hat. Note the circular mark on this cap; the same mark on the back provided identification markings for the other soldiers in a patrol. Around his neck is a sweat-rag, and he wears up-to-date canvas and rubber jungle boots. The 1944-type webbing pattern was made specifically for the Far East theatre in World War II.

Date:	1966
Unit:	7th Gurkha Rifles
Rank:	Rifleman
Location:	Bornean Jungle
Conflict:	Indonesian 'Confrontation'

Trooper
22 SAS Regiment
Oman 1973

The SAS often has considerable informality in its dress. This soldier in Oman in the 1970s has composed a uniform ideal for the hot and dry climate. He wears a khaki zip-fastened top with hood over a woollen jumper for warmth during the chilly desert nights, while the trousers are of an anonymous olive-drab battledress. His cap is a standard British Army jungle pack. Shoes have been sensibly selected from civilian sources, these being suede and much better adapted to hot climates than leather. His weapon is the powerful 7.62mm (0.3in) General Purpose Machine Gun made by the FN Herstal concern. One item that is worth reflection is the webbing. This is the SAS-designed Lightweight Combat Pack made from three packs hung by nylon mesh shoulder pieces, which gave 'breathability' in hot climates.

Date:	1973
Unit:	22 SAS Regiment
Rank:	Trooper
Location:	Oman
Conflict:	Guerrilla War, Oman

Lance-Corporal Parachute Regiment Londonderry 1980

A soldier pauses on the streets of Londonderry during a patrol in the early 1980s, a time when ambush and bomb detonations were everyday threats. Despite the enmity with which nationalist organizations held the Parachute Regiment, this soldier still wears the famous red beret, though note that the winged para badge is blacked out to prevent snipers using it as an aiming point. The rest of his uniform is typical of British Army soldiers at this time. He is wearing a DPM camouflage shirt with a pair of olive-green fatigues and leather, ankle-high para boots. His webbing is the 1958-pattern, though the 1980s saw an updated webbing introduced as the new SA80 rifle began to be issued. For this patrol he carries only ammunition for his L1A1 rifle and water. The final, and essential, items of this soldier's kit are the kevlar body armour and the two-way radio with the microphone attached to the flak-jacket collar.

Date:	1980
Unit:	Parachute Regiment
Rank:	Lance-Corporal
Location:	Londonderry
Conflict:	Northern Ireland

Trooper 22 SAS Iranian Embassy London 1980

This SAS soldier, in action during the hostage-rescue mission at the Iranian Embassy in May 1980, is wearing the most advanced urban-combat gear of the time. To reduce his visual signature inside a building he is dressed in a black, flame resistant combat overall; his head is covered by an S6 respirator for breathing in rooms choked by CS gas, smoke and munitions fumes. From beneath his smock comes his Armourshield GPV 25 body armour with groin protector. No kit is carried except weaponry. His main firearm is the 9mm Heckler & Koch MP5 submachine gun, which is noted for its reliability and accuracy, the two essentials of a hostage-rescue weapon. However, should the gun jam, he can rely on one of the two Browning Hi-Power 9mm pistols strapped to his thighs.

Date:	1980
Unit:	22 SAS Regiment
Rank:	Trooper
Location:	Iranian Embassy, London
Conflict:	Iranian Embassy Siege

Private
Intelligence Corps
United Kingdom
1980

This soldier of the Intelligence Corps shows us the new pattern uniforms which took the British Army soldier away from the olive-drab combat dress of the 1960s. He is wearing the 1968-pattern Combat Dress rendered in the No. 8 Temperate Disruptive Pattern Material (DPM) camouflage, which has become the British Army standard (DPM was introduced in 1972). The actual style of the uniform is the same as the earlier 1960-pattern and of the same fabric (sateen cotton gabardine drill, or cotton model fabrics) but as well as the DPM, it was lighter in construction, featured a pen pocket on the left sleeve, omitted the elbow reinforcements of the 1960 pattern, and had a standard shirt collar instead of the heavily stitched 'storm' collar. This soldier is wearing the 1958-pattern webbing and also the green beret of the Intelligence Corps.

Date:	1980
Unit:	Intelligence Corps
Rank:	Private
Location:	United Kingdom
Conflict:	None

Marine
Royal Marines
East Falkland 1982

The arctic climate encountered by British troops during the Falklands War tested British Army kit to the limit and revealed some deficiencies. Worst amongst these was the DMS (Directly Moulded Sole) boot, which had poor performance in constantly wet conditions and contributed to a high incidence of trench foot (this soldier wears waterproof boot-covers to increase the comfort). However, the other elements of this soldier's dress would have served him fairly well. The uniform is the 'Arctic Windproof Combat Smock and Trousers' rendered in Temperate Disruptive Pattern Material camouflage, the standard camouflage of the British Army. The smock had a large hood; when this included a wire stiffener, it was an 'RM pattern'; otherwise it was an 'SAS pattern'. The webbing is 1958-pattern, and his weapon is the L4A2, a 7.62mm (0.3in) version of the esteemed Bren.

Date:	1982
Unit:	Royal Marine
Rank:	Marine
Location:	East Falkland
Conflict:	Falklands War

Squadron Leader
No. 1 Squadron, RAF
HMS *Invincible* 1982

Harrier GR3 aircraft deployed from Royal Navy aircraft carriers made a seminal contribution to the Falklands War, launching ground-attack missions against Argentine positions and protecting the British Task Force fleet against anti-ship attacks. Here this RAF officer is seen in full flying gear. On the surface he wears an olive, one-piece flying overall which features clear plastic map pockets on the knees. Beneath is a Mk 10 immersion suit, which would increase survivability should he have to ditch in the freezing South Atlantic, as would the Mk 22 inflatable life-preserver, and also a compression suit to help cope with G-forces (the air supply to this is via the hose over the left hip). The blue straps around his legs would pin his legs tight during an ejection, and once landed the Personal Locator Beacon over his left breast would give rescue forces an exact location which they might be able to work towards.

Date:	1982
Unit:	No.1 Squadron, RAF
Rank:	Squadron Leader
Location:	HMS *Invincible*, South Atlantic
Conflict:	Falklands War

Rifleman
Gurkha Rifles
Western Europe
1980s

This Gurkha soldier is interesting for illustrating standard British Army dress as it generally exists today, rather than any distinctly Gurkha features. Though there has been an update in both uniform and webbing since the 1980s with the Combat 95 system, the format is still essentially the same as seen here. This Gurkha wears a 1984-pattern DPM camouflage combat uniform with 1958-pattern webbing (distinguished by the metal buckle instead of the plastic fittings of the modern Personal Load-Carrying Equipment). His helmet is the GS Combat Helmet Mk 6, made of ballistic nylon and featuring space over the ears to wear a communications headset beneath, and able to be worn with a respirator. His firearm is the 5.56mm (0.22in) L86 Light Support Weapon, a heavy-barrelled version of the standard SA80 rifle.

Date:	Late 1980s
Unit:	Gurkha Rifles
Rank:	Rifleman
Location:	Western Europe
Conflict:	None

Private
Parachute Regiment
Western Europe
1990s

Here we see a private of the Parachute Regiment dressed in the modern British Army uniform: the British Army Combat Soldier 1995 (CS95) system. CS95 works on a layering principle like most modern military uniforms and provides a range of different clothing items: a T-shirt, a lightweight combat shirt; a Norwegian pattern roll-neck overshirt; camouflaged fleece jacket; ripstop, weatherproof combat jacket and a fully waterproof, Gore-Tex outer jacket. The uniform had a new CS95 webbing system with more comfortable mesh strap systems and pouches made from heavy-duty, pressurized waterproof nylon. This soldier is carrying marching-order pack, including a heavy Bergen rucksack. He wears the famous red beret and carries the 5.56mm (0.22in) SA80 with a standard Sight Unit Small Arms Trilux (SUSAT) sight.

Date:	1990s
Unit:	Parachute Regiment
Rank:	Private
Location:	Western Europe
Conflict:	None

Mountain Leader M&AW Cadre Norway 1990s

The Mountain & Arctic Warfare Cadre (M&AW) is an élite unit within the Royal Marines which, as its name implies, specializes in combat and survival in mountainous or sub-zero environments. The demands on clothing in these climes is severe, and this soldier shows the typical survival gear (most of the M&AW training takes place in Norway, as the Royal Marines have a protective role in relation to NATO's northern flank). He is wearing a white, waterproof smock and trousers made from a 'breathable' fabric such as Gore-Tex over a windproof uniform. Thermal underwear forms the base layer of his clothing. Because exposed body-parts freeze in seconds in an arctic environment, body cover is almost total, and with a camouflaged M16A1 rifle, he would be hard to spot against snow. The gloves are specially designed for operation of the firearm.

Date:	1990s
Unit:	M&AW Cadre
Rank:	Mountain Leader
Location:	Norway
Conflict:	None

Private
US Army
Cuba 1902

The US occupation of Cuba from 1899 saw a khaki tropical dress introduced as standard uniform for lower ranks, yet most soldiers in the theatre wore a variation on the 1880 field dress. This consisted of a drab wide-brimmed hat worn with a blue shirt, blue grey trousers and brown leggings, the shoes being black. Kit was carried across the body in a blanket roll. This soldier conforms on the whole to the description, though there was much personalization of dress amongst the mainly volunteer units. The brown canvas trousers here are more in line with those worn by US cavalry troops. In 1902 a universal olive-drab uniform was issued throughout the US Army, by 1903 accompanied by a new form of webbing equipment which let the haversack, bayonet and entrenching tool hang from the belt. This soldier's rifle is the Springfield 1903, the original weapon which began four decades of Springfield production.

Date:	1902
Unit:	US Army
Rank:	Private
Theatre:	Cuba
Location:	Cuban posting

253

Lieutenant-Colonel 1st Cavalry Division Morocco 1942

Because of the rapidity with which the US was launched into World War II, many of its soldiers went into the early actions in quite dated uniforms (though from 1943 the US Army began to receive uniforms of far greater sophistication than their allies' equivalent). Here a lieutenant-colonel of the 1st Cavalry Division is wearing one such older style. His shirt and breeches are part of the 'Class C' uniform, this being the standard issue for troops operating in hot climates. They are made from khaki drill, or 'chino' as it was termed in the US, and are worn with a matching belt and distinctive field boots with buckled calf sections. These boots must have been an oddity by late 1942, as most were phased out before the US entered the war in December 1941. For headgear, this officer wears the classic broad-brimmed campaign hat, here featuring yellow cords to indicate the cavalry branch of the US Army.

Date:	November 1942
Unit:	1st Cavalry Division
Rank:	Lieutenant-Colonel
Theatre:	Mediterranean
Location:	Morocco

Captain
US Marine Corps
Iceland 1942

The uniform seen here began to be issued amongst the US Marines in 1929, finally settling the style of Marine Corps uniforms after about 17 years of redesign and adaptations. It consists of a single-breasted khaki-green jacket and matching pantaloons, here worn with the less common high lace-up boots. Insignia upon the jacket is simple: rank upon the shoulder straps (a officer's lanyard runs around the left shoulder), brass Marine Corps badges on the collar; a polar bear badge on the left sleeve to indicate the chilly Icelandic posting (guarding against any German invasion attempt), and, on a personal note, a French *Croix de Guerre* medal. This latter addition was a unit award to the 5th and 6th Marines for service in the French theatre in 1917–18. Prior to the early 1940s, webbing for the Marines tended to be leather, yet in 1942 this was changed to a cloth system. The helmet is the M1917 model.

Date:	January 1942
Unit:	US Marine Corps
Rank:	Captain
Theatre:	Atlantic
Location:	Iceland

US Marine
1st Marine
Defense Battalion
Wake Island 1941

The Marine Defense battalions were tasked with defending US Pacific interests, and this soldier is one of the 450 men who fought an incredibly brave action against Japanese invasion forces on Wake Island during December 1941. So early in the US entry into the war, the Marines uniform was conspicuously dated (Marines often lagged behind the uniform issue of other arms-of-service anyway). Here this Marine is wearing a World War I-pattern khaki shirt and trousers, with long, lace-up gaiters and a pair of brown leather shoes. His helmet is the M1917 helmet, modelled on that of the British Army. The large sack hanging over his left shoulder contains a gas mask. Though by this time production of the M1 Garand automatic rifle had begun, this soldier is still armed with the bolt-action M1903 Springfield rifle.

Date:	December 1941
Unit:	1st Marine Defense Battalion
Rank:	US Marine
Theatre:	Pacific
Location:	Wake Island

Gunnery Sergeant US Marine Corps Washington, USA 1941

The full dress uniform of the US Marines in World War II is shown here on this gunnery sergeant during duties in Washington. He wears a 'Dress Blue' tunic with standing collar, lighter blue trouser with a red stripe running down the outside edge of each leg, and white-and-blue dress peaked cap bearing the USMC crest (a US eagle and globe on top of a fouled anchor) in a brass badge. Rank on the Dress Blue uniform was rendered in gold on a red background on both sleeves until September 1942, after which it featured on the left arm only. The diagonal stripes below the rank are service stripes indicating 12 years of service (one stripe for each four years). The importance of marksmanship in the Marine Corps is suggested by the badges under the medal ribbon on the chest, the one on the left denoting an expert rifleman, and the other pistol proficiency.

Date:	December 1941
Unit:	Marine Corps
Rank:	Gunnery Sergeant
Theatre:	USA
Location:	Washington

Lieutenant US Navy Aviator USS *Enterprise* Central Pacific 1941

Carrier pilots in the US Navy had a grey-green service dress consisting of tunic with four patch pockets, matching trousers, and brown shoes, and they also had a khaki drill shirt and black tie. Such standard uniform is worn here by this lieutenant pilot aboard the USS *Enterprise* in the central Pacific Ocean. His rank is displayed by the black lace stripes and stars on his tunic sleeve, and also on the collar tips of the shirt (the climate of the Pacific demanded shirt sleeves for much of the day). The only other adornment on his tunic is the 1919-pattern Naval Aviator wings over his left breast. The peaked officer caps would match the uniform, and a white cover was available for full dress uniform. The peak is black, as is the badge background. Before May 1941 the badge eagle faced left; after this date, it faced right.

Date:	December 1941
Unit:	USS *Enterprise*
Rank:	Lieutenant
Theatre:	Pacific
Location:	Central Pacific Ocean

Staff-Sergeant 1st Infantry Division Oran 1942

Heavily burdened with equipment for the amphibious landings in Algeria, this staff-sergeant wears the olive-drab uniform donned by most US Army soldiers in the Mediterranean and North European (spring and summer) theatres. On his torso he has three layers. The base layer is an olive-drab wool shirt, this being covered by a lightweight field jacket which was waterproof, sand-coloured as opposed to olive-drab, and had a zip fastening with a buttoned fly front. On this he wears his rank on the right sleeve and the national flag on the left. Though it cannot be easily seen, this soldier is also wearing a life-jacket in case his landing craft is sunk. To match his upper half, the soldier has olive-drab trousers, the ankles being drawn in by long, elasticated anklets. The steel helmet is the US M1 and he wears the M1923 cartridge belt around his waist with two cotton ammunition bandoliers around his shoulders.

Date:	November 1942
Unit:	1st Infantry Division
Rank:	Staff-Sergeant
Theatre:	Mediterranean
Location:	Oran

Corporal
Tank Battalion
Morocco 1942

The standard of uniform for US armoured crews was consistently high, as is demonstrated by this corporal in the North African theatre in 1942. The basic uniform was a one-piece olive-drab overall made from herringbone twill. This featured four large utility pockets and a matching cloth belt to bring the overall in at the waist. Yet it was the additional items of the clothing which added comfort. This corporal wears the popular crewman's jacket. It was lightweight with a zip fastener, had two large waist slash pockets, an elasticated waistband and a knitted collar. Rank was displayed on the jacket via the sleeve. The helmet was another welcome US innovation. Made of fibre, it was incredibly tough and light, but holes bored through the dome gave welcome ventilation in the hot tank interior. On this soldier's right hip is a M1911 pistol and medical pouch, while on the right hip is an ammunition pouch.

Date:	November 1942
Unit:	Tank Battalion
Rank:	Corporal
Theatre:	Mediterranean
Location:	Morocco

Petty Officer 1st Class
Task Force 34
Atlantic Ocean 1942

This Task Force 34 sailor is seen during the Allied landings in North Africa (named Operation Torch) which began on 8 November 1942. As a rating, he can be seen wearing the standard navy-blue square rig uniform which consisted of blue pullover with white-striped flap collar, black knotted scarf, matching blue trousers, black shoes and white cap. His rank is displayed through the red chevrons on his left sleeve, above which is worn a radio speciality badge. The cuffs do not refer to rank, but to seaman grades, and the three stripes (120mm (4.7in) long with each stripe 5mm (0.2in) wide), joined together by vertical edge stripes, correspond with Seaman 3rd Class. The rest of the uniform remains unadorned. For cold-weather duties, US seaman were issued with a thick pea-coat, which was double-breasted with two rows of metal or plastic buttons with the US eagle displayed on them.

Date:	November 1942
Unit:	Task Force 34
Rank:	Petty Officer 1st Class
Theatre:	Mediterranean
Location:	Atlantic Ocean

Corporal
US Army
Military Police
England 1942

A corporal of the Military Police directs personnel at a base in England in 1942. The uniform he is wearing is a standard khaki US Army uniform of the 1940s, though here it is worn with MP additions. The basic uniform is a khaki, single-breasted tunic with an open fall collar and two breast- and two side patch pockets with matching trousers. Beneath the tunic is a khaki shirt with lighter olive-drab tie, this replacing the earlier black version in February 1942. Military Police were nicknamed 'snow drops' by regular troops on account of their white additions to the standard uniform, including the anklets, web belt, gloves, lanyard and helmet, and the letters 'MP' featured in white on the left sleeve. Rank is indicated on the upper sleeves by 80mm (3.2in) wide chevrons rendered in khaki silk or stitched in yellow onto a blue gabardine patch.

Date:	December 1942
Unit:	US Army Military Police
Rank:	Corporal
Theatre:	North-west Europe
Location:	London, England

Pilot
US Marine Corps
Bougainville
1943

The Marine Corps contributed over 10,000 aviators in 128 squadrons to Allied forces in World War II, the majority of them operating in support of the US push through the islands of the Pacific against the Japanese. The scorching and humid Pacific climate is reflected in this pilot's dress. He wears a one-piece tropical flight overall made in a light khaki cotton with a zip fastener. As a Marine Corps pilot he wears a matching infantry M1943 web belt. The equipment hanging from this belt is, from left hip to right hip, a water bottle in its button cover, a pouch containing two magazines for a Colt .45in M1911 pistol and finally a pouch containing some basic field dressings. Functional clothing is worn in the shape of a yellow, inflatable life-jacket, a leather flying helmet, and flying goggles with tinted glass.

Date:	June 1943
Unit:	US Marine Corps
Rank:	Pilot
Theatre:	Pacific
Location:	Bougainville

Marine
2nd Marine Division
Tarawa 1943

The battle of Tarawa was one of the bloodiest episodes in the history of the Marine Corps, which saw a total of nearly 1000 Marines killed on a central island less than 4km (2.5 miles) long. By contrast, however, of the 4500 Japanese defenders, only 17 were left alive. This soldier is wearing the two-piece herringbone-twill uniform which became the dominant dress code of US Marines in the Pacific theatre, along with the coarser 'dungaree' uniform. Both these style of uniforms featured a single patch pocket over the left breast, and this had the letters 'USMC' and the Marines crest stencilled in black on its surface. His M1 helmet is camouflaged with a 'beach' pattern cover, and this pattern evolved into being a full uniform by 1945. The M1943 web belt supports six ammunition pouches for his M1 Garand rifle, each pouch holding two five-round clips.

Date:	November 1943
Unit:	2nd Marine Division
Rank:	Marine
Theatre:	Pacific
Location:	Tarawa

Petty Officer 3rd Class USS *Saratoga* The Solomons 1943

This sailor presents an interesting counterpoint to the usual appearance of personnel aboard US ships during the war. The awesome logistical demands on the US Navy during the Pacific conflict meant that tens of thousands of foreign ship-crew were recruited into the service to provide functions such as cooking, cleaning, and administration. The sailor shown here, Samoan by origin, is employed on the USS *Saratoga* as a cook, this job being identified by the US eagle badge with a 'C' underneath on his lava-lava (the wrapped skirt around his waist). Apart from this, he bears little resemblance to US ship personnel, his uniform further consisting of a red waist-sash, white T-shirt and red turban. Auxiliary crew were known to contribute to the Allied cause with extreme bravery, as shown by the Purple Heart ribbon on this sailor's left breast.

Date:	November 1943
Unit:	USS *Saratoga*
Rank:	Petty Officer 3rd Class
Theatre:	Pacific
Location:	The Solomons

Captain
7th Air Force
USAAF
Hawaii 1944

The Pacific theatre presented harsh climactic challenges for bomber crews, from tropical temperatures at ground level to freezing temperatures at high altitudes. This was more so once Pacific islands close to Japan were captured and long-range, high-altitude area bombing of the Japanese mainland began. Visible at the ankle here is the beige trousers of the air-force drill dress, worn on ground duties or beneath operational clothing. Over this is the Shearling flying suit: a B-3 fur-lined jacket and A-3 fur-lined trousers, both items being zip-fastened with long zips for convenience of removal and to provide selected ventilation at varying altitudes. The headgear is the B-2 flying cap with flaps and more fur lining.

Date:	January 1944
Unit:	7th Air Force
Rank:	Captain
Theatre:	Pacific
Location:	Hawaii

Sergeant Grade 4 101st Airborne Division Normandy 1944

The US Army originally had two NCO ranks – corporal and sergeant – but a few years into World War II and the sergeant rank had five subdivisions. It was not always possibly to tell the rank of sergeant by the chevrons, though technician NCOs often had a small 'T' within the chevrons. This soldier is a sergeant, grade 4, and he is dressed in the specially designed para uniform introduced into airborne forces in the early 1940s. The standard jump-uniform was a two-piece, olive-green tunic and trousers, the latter featuring reinforced sections on the knees. Instead of a dedicated para helmet, he wears the standard M1, introduced in 1941 to replace the British-pattern helmet. All his webbing is worn over the uniform, with loose equipment bound in with webbing tape, and he holds the folding-stock para version of the .30 calibre M1A1 carbine.

Date:	June 1944
Unit:	101st Airborne Division
Rank:	Sergeant Grade 4
Theatre:	North-west Europe
Location:	Normandy

Lieutenant US Army England 1944

A US Army lieutenant takes a drink just prior to embarking for the D-Day landings on Omaha and Utah beaches. It was common practice in the US Army to paint officer's rank markings on the front of the helmet, despite the threat from snipers. Over his M1941 combat jacket and olive fatigues he wears a mass of equipment for the amphibious landings. The half-inflated pouch centred over his chest is a flotation bag, intended to provide some protection from drowning during the landings. Beneath the bag is an officer's dispatch case containing maps of his objectives. The main priority in equipment apart from these two items is ammunition. He wears a special combat waistcoat with integral ammunition pockets in addition to his standard belt-hung pouches. His armament is the M1 carbine – here seen slung over the shoulder – and a Colt .45 M1911 pistol in a leather holster on the right hip.

Date:	5 June 1944
Unit:	US Army
Rank:	Lieutenant
Theatre:	North-west Europe
Location:	Southern England

Major-General 82nd Airborne Division Europe 1944

The major-general seen here is wearing the M1944 field jacket, popularly known as the 'Ike' jacket, after General Eisenhower, the Allied invasion commander. His membership of the 82nd Airborne is denoted by several elements of insignia on this jacket, most distinctly the army paratrooper badge on the left breast, mirrored by a further para badge up on the cap (white set on a navy-blue background). Also featured on the jacket are an infantry combat badge (left breast, beneath the decoration ribbons), a unit citation badge on the right breast, this being made of blue and silver enamel and issued after 15 November 1943, and the double-A badge of the 82nd on the left sleeve. Rank is indicated by the stripes on the cuff and the stars on the shoulder straps and cap. The cap, a special overseas version, also has gold piping to indicate his general status.

Date:	May 1944
Unit:	82nd Airborne Division
Rank:	Major-General
Theatre:	North-west Europe
Location:	England

Ensign
US Atlantic Fleet
Washington 1944

The US saw much naval action in the Pacific, but it also had a major commitment to the Atlantic theatre in convoy protection and U-boat hunting. Here we see a US naval ensign (the lowest commissioned rank). The solider is dated by the length of the rank stripes on the cuff: before 1 January 1944, they looped around the entire cuff; after this they extended across only the outside half of the sleeve. The star on the cuff indicates line-officer status. An ensign might also have rank displayed on shoulder-straps (one gold lace ring) or shirt collar and side cap (one metal bar). The general uniform here is the standard navy-blue officer's service dress with double-breasted jacket and two rows of gilt buttons, white shirt and black tie, and white-covered service cap with the navy badge, black strap and gold band, and a black leather peak. The aiguillette and braid on the shoulder was worn by presidential aides.

Date:	June 1944
Unit:	US Atlantic Fleet
Rank:	Ensign
Theatre:	Atlantic
Location:	Washington

Officer
US Women's
Army Corps
Pearl Harbor 1944

This US servicewoman is wearing the cotton summer uniform issued to personnel of the US Women's Army Corps during World War II. It consisted of a dark-olive tunic with open collar, broad lapels, and gilt buttons with a matching peaked cap. Underneath the tunic was worn a light khaki blouse and tie. A khaki skirt and a pair of brown leather shoes completed the uniform. The WAC had their own system of insignia. The cap badge was an American eagle, usually less adorned than the standard US Army cap badge, though this officer actually has the regular cap badge with the scroll and motto 'E Pluribus Unum'. WACs had the letters 'US' on the upper collar and the head of the Greek goddess Pallas Athene (goddess of war) beneath. Rank would be shown on the shoulder-straps and, for officers, through the contrasting olive ribbon around the cuff.

Date:	June 1944
Unit:	US Women's Army Corps
Rank:	Officer
Theatre:	Pacific
Location:	Pearl Harbor

Captain
8th Army Air Force
England 1944

By mid-1944 the Allied bombing campaign against the German heartland had round-trip escort in the form of US Mustang fighter aircraft equipped with long-range drop tanks. This took away German fighter superiority at the target of a mission and thus increased the effectiveness of Allied bombing runs. The captain here is the pilot of one such P-51B Mustang, seen here at the fighter base back in East Anglia. He is wearing typically informal USAAF fighter pilot uniform. Standard drill uniform was olive-drab trousers, with light khaki tunic and matching shirt and tie, though for flying a fleece-lined leather jacket was worn over the shirt with matching leather trousers. Here only the leather jacket is worn, with a yellow life-jacket over the top and a khaki field cap instead of the fleece-lined flying helmet. The boots are the A-6 pattern fur-lined overboots which were zipped over the standard brown shoes of USAAF personnel.

Date:	July 1944
Unit:	8th Army Air Force
Rank:	Captain
Theatre:	North-west Europe
Location:	East Anglia

Aircrewman 8th Army Air Force East Anglia 1944

This aircrewman is fitting himself with the 'flak suit' designed by Brigadier-General Grow and manufactured by the Wilkinson Sword company. The flak suit was introduced from 1943 in an attempt to deal with the shrapnel injuries to bomber crews resulting from exploding anti-aircraft shells. It came in two pieces, one to provide torso protection, the other to shield the wearer's groin and abdomen. The actual armour weighed some 9kg (20lb) and consisted of cloth-wrapped manganese steel plates which could firmly stop all but the largest pieces of high-velocity shrapnel (they were tested with .45in pistol rounds at almost point-blank range). Though bulky, the reassurance provided by the armour made it popular amongst crews. Apart from the armour, this aircrewman is wearing olive-green flying overalls – the alternative to the khaki shirt, trouser and tunic – with a peaked USAAF cap.

Date:	July 1944
Unit:	8th Army Air Force
Rank:	Aircrewman
Theatre:	North-west Europe
Location:	East Anglia

Private 101st Airborne Division Belgium 1944

US soldiers facing the winter in northern Europe in 1944/5 were lucky that the issue of M1943 combat uniforms had begun. This uniform utilized an advanced (for the time) layering principle, whereby the soldier could combine a waterproof and windproof jacket and overtrousers with additional layers of warm clothing. However, by November 1944 the issue of this uniform was not complete, as is evident for this soldier with the M1943 jacket (distinguished from the older M1941 jacket by chest patch pockets) but also older khaki woollen service trousers. He has rubber waterproof covers for his leather combat boots, these having snap fastenings, and carries a variety of equipment and acquisitions, including an M1 Garand rifle, a cooking pot hung from his belt and an entrenching tool around the left hip.

Date:	November 1944
Unit:	101st Airborne Division
Rank:	Private
Theatre:	North-west Europe
Location:	Belgium

Bomber Crewman 8th Army Air Force England 1945

This aviator is a crewman aboard a B-17 Flying Fortress. B-17s were the key US long-range strategic bombers in all theatres except the Pacific, where the B-29 Superfortress was responsible for most of the significant raids against the Japanese mainland. The B-17s bore the brunt of the US policy of daylight bombing against Germany, this policy being altered after hideous losses on the Schweinfurt raid (14 October 1943) but reinvigorated with the introduction of long-range fighter escorts in 1944. This B-17 crewman is preparing for take-off in early 1945. He is wearing a one-piece flying suit lined with wool and alpaca, over this donning an olive-drab flying jacket with a formation badge on the sleeve. Extra warmth is provided by fleece-lined gloves and zip-on overboots. Headgear consists of an A-11 leather helmet, B-8 flying goggles and an A-10 oxygen mask to cope with altitudes of more than 8534m (28,000ft).

Date:	February 1945
Unit:	8th Army Air Force
Rank:	Bomber Crewman
Theatre:	North-west Europe
Location:	East Anglia

Marine
US Marine Corps
Inchon 1950

Deployed to Korea only five years after the end of World War II, this Marine at the Inchon amphibious landings in 1950 is kitted out in gear worn mainly by US servicemen during the Pacific campaigns. His main uniform items are a set of olive-drab M1944 fatigues in a herringbone-twill material, these being defined by the longitudinal pattern of the cloth, the two large patch pockets on the trousers, and also the single patch pocket over the left breast with the USMC letters and badge stencilled in black. His helmet is the US M1 with the 'beach' camouflage cover, which was worn extensively during the Pacific war. He is carrying ammunition for his M1 .30in calibre rifle in his M1923 cartridge belt and also in the cotton bandoliers across his chest, around 200 rounds in total. Visible over his left shoulder is the handle of his bayonet positioned for easy access to use in hand-to-hand combat situations.

Date:	September 1950
Unit:	1st Marine Division
Rank:	Marine
Theatre:	Inchon
Location:	Korean War

Private
US Airborne Forces
38th Parallel 1951

Though this soldier wears the waterproof and windproof M1943 trousers, he has yet to be issued with the jacket and instead wears the older pattern M1941 jacket (this did not have the patch pockets of the M1943). His webbing and kit is arranged very much in battle order, and he appears heavily armed. For his M1 Garand rifle he carries ammunition in a six-pouch rifleman's belt with a single quick-release buckle. The small pouch which hangs beneath the belt on the left hip is a first-aid pouch, while emergency dressings are taped to the left shoulder-strap for easy access in combat. He also has an M1943 entrenching tool around the back alongside a kidney pouch. Additional weaponry is seen in the form of a Colt M1911 pistol and fighting knife. With his M1 helmet he looks like most other members of the US Army in Korea, though his 'Corcoran' parachute boots are uniquely airborne issue.

Date:	1951
Unit:	US Airborne Forces
Rank:	Private
Location:	Around the 38th Parallel
Conflict:	Korean War

Captain 5th Special Forces Group Vietnam 1965

This Special Forces captain – part of the Civilian Irregular Defense Group (CIDG) programme training South Vietnamese ethnic groups to fight the Viet Cong – is wearing the standard olive-green fatigues worn by most US soldiers in the early part of the Vietnam War. This initial pattern had slanting patch pockets on the shirt and exposed buttons, as opposed to later patterns which had horizontal pockets and covered buttons to prevent snagging on undergrowth. However, many SP personnel also wore camouflage outfits, particularly the 'Tigerstripe' pattern, which almost became a definer of élite units. His headgear is a green beret with rank bars imposed on the badge (rank bars are also on the right collar). The webbing is the M1956 Load-Carrying Equipment, with an ammunition pack for his .30in M2 Carbine. His boots are canvas-and-leather jungle issue.

Date:	1965
Unit:	5th SPG
Rank:	Captain
Location:	South Vietnam
Conflict:	Vietnam War

Trooper US 1st Air Cavalry Division South Vietnam 1966

As was usual for US personnel in Vietnam at this time, this soldier is wearing the standard green fatigues. The pockets are of the later horizontal, rather than diagonal, format, though he is still in the old leather boots, prone to rot in the jungle, rather than the jungle boots which were issued from 1965. What is more interesting is how this soldier illustrates the typical gear of a soldier on search-and-destroy missions. He is very heavily armed, with the three bags suspended from his left shoulder, each carrying a Claymore directional anti-personnel mine. The pouch to his right on the M1956 web belt holds magazines for his M16A1 rifle, while the belt also holds two fragmentation grenades. Personal items include a water bottle on his right hip and the obligatory insect repellent stuck in his hat band.

Date:	1966
Unit:	1st Air Cavalry
Rank:	Trooper
Location:	South Vietnamese Highlands
Conflict:	Vietnam War

Private 1st Class US Marine Corps Hue 1968

The Tet Offensive of 1968, during which North Vietnam launched its first full-scale invasion of the South, introduced the US Marine Corps to major urban warfare during the epic battle to reclaim the ancient city of Hue. This private 1st class is armed with an M60 machine gun and heavily kitted out, indicative of the fact that the fighting in Hue went on for nearly a month. The basic uniform of Marines in Vietnam was the same as that of the Army, though with the letters 'USMC' over the left breast pocket. Though Marines tended towards older kit issues, this soldier has modern equipment in his M1956 webbing. His plastic water bottles are the latest issue (previously the water bottles were black enamel), next to which a medical pouch is hung from the belt. At the top of his pack are waterproofs. As a seasonal touch, he carries a miniature Christmas tree.

Date:	January 1968
Unit:	USMC
Rank:	Private 1st Class
Location:	Hue
Conflict:	Vietnam War

Sergeant
US Special Forces
Cambodian Border
1968

Camouflage uniforms tended to be the preserve of Special Forces or operatives during the Vietnam War, especially those personnel making deep-penetration missions into enemy territory or, as in this case, skirting close to the Cambodian border. However, his mission is probably of a non-sensitive nature, as he wears Special Forces insignia on his arm (such insignia would usually be left off in case of capture). The badge consists of a Fairborn commando knife crossed by three lightning flashes, each flash indicating specialisms on land, at sea, and in an airborne capacity. The Woodland camouflage was issued to élite units from 1967; in the early years in Vietnam many Special Forces soldiers would buy camouflage hunting clothes. He wears the nylon-and-leather jungle boots and an M1956 webbing system.

Date:	1968
Unit:	US Special Forces
Rank:	Sergeant
Location:	Cambodian Border
Conflict:	Vietnam War

Corporal
US Marine Corps
St George's 1983

This corporal, seen here during the US invasion of Grenada in 1983, is wearing a mixture of the old and the new. What is new for the time is the pattern of camouflage: M81 Woodland. As its numbering suggests, the M81 began to be printed on US uniforms from the early 1980s, and it provided a good, general-purpose camouflage for temperate and tropical environments. Of older issue is the helmet, the steel M1. By 1983, many US soldiers were equipped with the new kevlar helmet. His webbing is the ALICE system – All-Purpose Lightweight Individual Carrying Equipment – which was introduced during the 1970s. His weapon is the potent M60 machine gun, here with a box feed to enable it to be operated easily by one man.

Date:	1983
Unit:	US Marine Corps
Rank:	Corporal
Location:	St George's, Grenada
Conflict:	US invasion of Grenada

Sergeant
US 75th Infantry
(Ranger) Regiment
Grenada 1983

The US Rangers were deployed on some of the most dangerous missions of the Grenadan invasion. We see this soldier at Port Salines holding the 5.56mm (0.22in) M4 Carbine with a collapsible stock. He wears OD twill jungle fatigues with a matching field cap and nylon-and-leather jungle boots. His field cap has luminous identification patches for low-light conditions. Rank is displayed by three metal bars on the collar point. With his ALICE webbing, he wears an LC-2 equipment belt, on which are water bottles, combat knife and ammunition pouch.

Date:	1983
Unit:	US 75th Infantry (Ranger) Regiment
Rank:	Sergeant
Location:	Port Salines Airfield
Conflict:	US invasion of Grenada

Corporal
US Marine Corps
Quantico 1985

A Marine corporal shown here on parade in Quantico, the USMC headquarters, wears the Dress Blue B uniform which was donned mainly for ceremonial and official functions. The uniform's primary item is a dark-blue tunic which had a stand collar and is trimmed in red, worn with a white belt. On the cuff are service stripes – one stripe for every four years of service – while higher up the sleeve the rank is indicated in yellow on a red field. Metal USMC badges can be seen on the collar, and this soldier also has two meritorious unit citations displayed in ribbons on the left breast, with rifle and pistol proficiency badges attached underneath them. The trousers he is wearing are a lighter blue, and NCO ranks and higher have a red stripe down each leg. The cap is known as the Service Dress cap, with a white top, again featuring the USMC badge and a black leather strap, as well as a black peak.

Date:	1985
Unit:	US Marine Corps
Rank:	Corporal
Location:	Quantico, US
Conflict:	None

Private 1st Class US 82nd Airborne Division United States 1990s

This soldier of the 82nd Airborne presents a modern view of the US Army soldier. He is wearing items camouflaged in the General Purpose (Woodland) pattern issued to most US soldiers, this mixing foliage colours with sand colours for a greater versatility of terrain application. The helmet and the body armour belong to the Personal Armor System, Ground Troops (PASGT) which is based on kevlar ballistic protection and provides good protection against small arms and shell splinters. Equipment here – supported by the ALICE load-carrying system – includes an ammunition pouch, a smoke-grenade, and radio communications. The 82nd Airborne is one of the US Army's most prestigious units. Identification with this unit on combat uniforms usually comes in the form of an 'AA' (All American) divisional patch on the sleeve.

Date:	1990s
Unit:	82nd Airborne Division
Rank:	Private 1st Class
Location:	United States
Conflict:	None

Private
Russian Army
Russia 1916

The basic pattern of the World War I Russian Army uniform was established in 1907 after clothing trials following the Russo-Japanese war of 1904–05. The pattern chosen was an olive-green uniform of Gimnastirka shirt (non-officer ranks) or Kitel tunic (officers) with a woollen or cloth peaked cap and Shinel greatcoat. While the double-breasted greatcoat had a large fall collar, the tunic had a stand collar. Rank was placed on the shoulder-straps, and the greatcoat collar was used to receive coloured patches which indicated arm-of-service and regiment. This pattern received some variation in 1913, particularly the tunic which was modified with a rear vent and a different button configuration, giving it the feature of being able to act as both service and dress uniform. Service dress was achieved by buttoning a coloured plastron on the front of the tunic and altering cuff- and collar insignia.

Date:	1916
Unit:	Russian Army
Rank:	Private
Theatre:	Eastern Front
Location:	Western Russia

Seaman
Northern Fleet
Red Navy
Archangel 1939

The rating pictured here is wearing the standard uniform for a Russian seaman operating in the sub-zero climes of the Arctic Circle. Over a square rig outfit (dark-blue jumper and black, bell-bottomed trousers; the Russians were the only navy to mix black and blue) he dons a long, blue greatcoat issued for winter use, this ultimately replacing the pea-coat. This greatcoat was single-breasted with six yellow metal buttons, tied at the waist with a naval belt with anchor and star buckle, while the red star on the cuff indicates the rank of rating. The cap badge also features a red star with yellow hammer-and-sickle centred, and a yellow-and-black border, this being the rank display for rating to petty officer. Further cap details include the name of the ship's crew of Northern Fleet on the tally (in Cyrillic). The boots are winter issue, made from felt.

Date:	September 1939
Unit:	Northern Fleet
Rank:	Seaman
Theatre:	Arctic
Location:	Archangel

Colonel Armoured Division Red Army Kiev 1940

The steel-grey uniform here, the standard-issue service dress for Soviet armoured soldiers from 1935, replaced the khaki service dress worn by the rest of the infantry. It is a simple uniform of tunic and matching trousers, a peaked service cap, and a white shirt and black tie worn underneath. On the tunic shown here, there is very little in the way of insignia or badges. The rank is displayed in the chevrons on the cuffs – red with gold edging – and also on the metal and enamel badges on the collar patches. This system of rank was formed by the Revolutionary government, and all rank units were made up of a combination of red squares, triangles and diamonds. Colour was also used to represent military units; there were no regimental badges. The final Communist touch is the hammer-and-sickle badge on the peaked cap.

Date:	January 1940
Unit:	Armoured Division
Rank:	Colonel
Theatre:	Eastern Front
Location:	Kiev

Marshal of the Soviet Union Red Army Moscow 1940

Having risen rapidly through the military ranks, Marshal Timoshenko was awarded a Hero of the Soviet Union award and then rose to the status of Commander-in-Chief of the Soviet Armed Forces. Here we see him wearing the grey parade uniform of senior officers issued from 1940: a steel-grey tunic with red piping and a stand-and-fall collar, navy-blue pantaloons with the red piping of marshals and generals, knee-high riding boots and a peaked service cap in grey with a red band, two gold cords (marshals and generals) and black leather peak. As was customary for officers, rank is displayed on the sleeves and collar: a gold star surmounting a laurel wreath. Timonshenko's decorations are (top to bottom): Gold Star of a Hero of the Soviet Union, two Orders of Lenin, three Orders of the Red Banner, Red Army 20th Anniversary medal.

Date:	June 1940
Unit:	Kiev Military District
Rank:	Marshal of the Soviet Union
Theatre:	Eastern Front
Location:	Moscow

Major
Red Army Air Force
Kiev 1940

As part of the Red Army, the Russian Air Force during World War II was basically dressed as army personnel, though with some key differences of colouration. The air-force colour was blue, and this colour also featured on the cap band, the collar patches and the piping on the cuffs and trousers. Before the war, the air force's entire uniform was issued in a blue colour (introduced in December 1924), but as the years went on, this uniform became walking-out dress and the army's khaki tunic and breeches took over (this officer is mixing elements of the two styles). Rank in the air force was via gold and red chevrons on the sleeve (a system introduced in 1935). The two red enamelled rectangles on the collar patches also show rank, while the gold propeller naturally indicates the air force. The cap badges were a hammer-and-sickle set in a laurel wreath, above which was a wing and star symbol.

Date:	June 1940
Unit:	Red Army Air Force
Rank:	Major
Theatre:	Eastern Front
Location:	Kiev

Sergeant Cavalry Division Kiev 1941

While the top half of this soldier's uniform is essentially that of any other Red Army infantryman during the early years of the war, the blue pantaloons and black riding boots set him apart as a cavalryman. Another item which distinguishes him is the ceremonial cavalry sabre slung from his belt. The tunic and peaked service cap are standard Soviet Army issue, though the collar on the tunic is a stand collar, whereas the usual form was a stand-and-fall collar. Cuffs on this pattern of tunic featured two small buttons. The collar here has the rank depicted on a blue field, the colour of the cavalry units. This blue colour is repeated up on the cap band, on which is sited the Communist Star with hammer-and-sickle imposed in the middle in gold. This sergeant has minimal equipment, including a small ammunition pouch for a Nagant pistol which sits over his right hip, while behind his left hip can be seen a leather map case.

Date:	June 1941
Unit:	Cavalry Division
Rank:	Sergeant
Theatre:	Eastern Front
Location:	Kiev

Corporal
Infantry Division
Ukraine 1941

Though the Soviets coped better with the harsh Russian winters than their German adversaries, they still suffered from problems of substandard clothing. The Russian infantry uniform was extremely basic, as seen on the corporal here on the Ukrainian Front in the early months of Barbarossa. Over a khaki tunic and trousers, this soldier wears the standard infantry greatcoat. It was made of cheap cloth with variable production quality; the colour often varies between, and even within, garments from brown and grey. Officer greatcoats often had arm-of-service piping. The coat was fly-fronted and had a large fall collar on which were sited the rank patches; the black stripe indicates the rank of corporal, while the red background shows arm-of-service. His webbing system is made of leather, and the ammunition pouches are for one of history's earliest effective assault rifles: the Tokarev M1940.

Date:	July 1941
Unit:	Infantry Division
Rank:	Corporal
Theatre:	Eastern Front
Location:	Ukraine

Trooper
Cavalry Regiment
Leningrad 1941

This outlandish figure illustrates one of the more bizarre uniform configurations of World War II. The Soviet Union – particularly around the Leningrad Front, where this soldier is pictured – has many areas laced with waterways. These made mobility for both sides difficult, but a special kit was issued to some Russian soldiers to enable them to negotiate streams and rivers. As seen here, the outfit consisted of a large, inflatable rubber ring strapped around the waist, complete with harness straps, this having a set of waders attached through an integral fitting. Once the soldier was floating, he would use the small oars to propel himself, while the long rod he carries in his right hand was used to fathom out the depth of the water. The practicality of such gear is questionable, and even a moderate current could easily lead to the soldier being washed away.

Date:	October 1941
Unit:	Cavalry Regiment
Rank:	Trooper
Theatre:	Eastern Front
Location:	Leningrad

Officer
Infantry Division
Red Army
Moscow 1941

This soldier is pictured during the Red Army's dramatic push against the German forces around Moscow during the bitter winter of 1941/2. While the German forces ground to a halt, with many soldiers still wearing summer-issue uniforms, the Russians generally possessed clothing adapted from centuries of enduring such weather. This officer is kitted out in superb winter clothing of the type issued from 1941 (though it must be acknowledged that not all Russian infantry were as well dressed). The jacket and trousers – known together as the telogreika uniform – are made from a double layer of khaki material with cotton wool stitched in strips inside to provide a warming quilted effect. The valenki felt boots were also excellent winter wear, as they did not crack and avoided the problem of leather, which conducts heat away from the body.

Date:	December 1941
Unit:	Infantry Division
Rank:	Officer
Theatre:	Eastern Front
Location:	West of Moscow

Petty Officer 2nd Class Caspian Flotilla Black Sea 1943

This petty officer of the Caspian fleet wears the black-and-blue square rig uniform of the Red Navy. It is typical navy clothing: a black jumper with blue jean collar (a forminka) white striped, over a blue-and-white T-shirt, naval belt, black, bell-bottomed trousers and black shoes (petty officers of more than five years' service could also wear the navy peaked cap). This petty officer has a black-and- orange guard tally, awarded for a good service record, which extends down the back of his neck and features a foul anchor. Further evidence of solid service is in the campaign medal on his left breast. Gone are the rank markings on the sleeve, these being relocated up to the shoulder-straps in 1943. Petty officer badges featured one to three bars for 1st to 3rd class respectively, with a Cyrillic abbreviation above designating the fleet.

Date:	June 1943
Unit:	Caspian Flotilla
Rank:	Petty Officer 2nd Class
Theatre:	Eastern Front
Location:	Black Sea

295

Tankman
II Guards
Tank Corps
Kursk 1943

Though the colour of tankcrew uniforms varied through black, blue, grey and (as seen here) khaki, the style was fundamentally unchanged throughout the war. The standard uniform for wear during operations was a one-piece overall worn over the standard tunic and trousers, this overall featuring a single, large chest pocket and one on the thigh, plus two slash pockets, one on each side. Fastening for the overall was either a zip or through four front buttons, and the collar was of a soft-fall variety. Like the infantry uniform, the cuffs of this overall were fastened by two buttons. The soldier here wears the overall with high leather boots and a Sam Browne belt. The crash helmet was made of padded leather, and the buckles at the side allowed access to ear sections in which communications speakers could be inserted.

Date:	July 1943
Unit:	II Guards Tank Corps
Rank:	Tankman
Theatre:	Eastern Front
Location:	Kursk

Sniper Rifle Battalion Red Army Kursk 1943

Because of chronic problems in finding the manpower to fulfil military and industrial tasks, the Soviet Government recruited some 7.75 million women, of whom 800,000 served in the military. Sniping was a precision role which many women soldiers performed with expertise. Here we see a female sniper deployed around Kursk in July 1943. Soviet snipers were issued with one-piece specialist overalls to wear over their standard uniforms. However, during the war these uniforms were often camouflaged, especially for snipers. This overall has a khaki base with green foliage patterns. A large hood and soft cap would obscure the face in a position of hiding. Some overalls had strips of cloth sown to the shoulders and sleeves to break up the silhouette. This sniper's killing tool is the 7.62mm (0.3in) Mosin-Nagant M1891/30 rifle.

Date:	July 1943
Unit:	Rifle Battalion
Rank:	Sniper
Theatre:	Eastern Front
Location:	Kursk

General Red Army Moscow 1945

In essence this uniform is not a World War II issue, as it was produced for the celebrations and ceremonies following the defeat of Germany in May 1945. Moving away from the khaki, blues and steel-greys of earlier uniforms, the new full-dress uniform for generals and marshals was sea-green in colour. The tunic followed a sweeping, double-breasted design, almost entirely crossing the chest and having two rows of gilt buttons, each button showing the emblem of the Soviet Union. The tunic is extensively decorated. Laurel leaves are embroidered on the collar and cuffs, the cuffs also having three gold rings to signify general rank. The shoulder boards – gold with red edging – also show the rank of general through four gold stars. The red cap band indicates general of the army, while blue was the colour for the air force and black for the artillery.

Date:	May 1945
Unit:	Red Army
Rank:	General
Theatre:	Eastern Front
Location:	Moscow

Private
Soviet Infantry
Budapest 1956

Despite World War II being over for some 11 years, there is little except the firearm to distinguish this soldier from his wartime counterparts. Indeed, this style of uniform dominated Soviet infantry dress until well into the 1960s, a replacement uniform only filtering in about 1970. Here we see a khaki tunic with an uncomfortable-looking stand collar and shoulder-straps for the rank insignia, and khaki trousers tucked into black boots. The field cap displays the Communist Star in the centre. Two pouches are carried: the bag suspended around his neck carries a gas mask, while the pouch on his left hip holds ammunition. The weapon is the legendary AK-47 folding-stock version (strict title the AKS-47), the standard Soviet infantry rifle issue from 1948. It was a simple, solid weapon with absolute reliability. The solider here is pictured during the Soviet operation to quench the Hungarian Uprising.

Date:	1956
Unit:	Soviet Infantry
Rank:	Private
Location:	Budapest
Conflict:	Hungarian Uprising

Tank Driver Soviet Armoured Forces Prague 1968

By the late 1960s Soviet tank crews were wearing a two-piece black uniform as their operational clothing (here worn over the standard Soviet Army infantry tunic and trousers), though this later became a one-piece overall similar to the type worn by Russian tankmen during World War II. The uniform and the overall were unmarked, the rank markings residing on shoulder boards on the infantry tunic (black with the gold letters 'CA', and gold rank markings for armoured regiments, normal infantry boards for Motor Rifle Regiments). Head protection comes from the padded leather helmet, this featuring built-in communications. The socket for a RT/IC radio-to-vehicle transmitter is hanging down his left shoulder, while around his neck is a throat microphone. This type of uniform was also worn by the crew of armoured personnel carriers.

Date:	1968
Unit:	Soviet Armoured Regiment
Rank:	Driver
Location:	Prague
Conflict:	Invasion of Czechoslovakia

Paratrooper Soviet Airborne Forces Kabul 1979

This paratrooper is seen at the beginning of the Soviet Union's invasion of Afghanistan in 1979, part of the large waves of Guards Airborne Divisions used to capture airfields and other significant targets around Kabul. As élite soldiers — indicated by the blue-and-white striped T-shirt worn by all Soviet special forces — they were used heavily throughout the 10-year occupation of the country, performing aggressive search-and-destroy operations against remote Mujahedeen strongholds. Here the paratrooper is wearing a one-piece padded jumpsuit to give protection from the harsh Afghan climate, though on the ground the standard infantry uniform would be worn by para soldiers. A leather head-protector is worn; a helmet was worn over it during jumps. The leather webbing supports a utility pouch (left) and a 9mm APS pistol (right).

Date:	1979
Unit:	Soviet Airborne Forces
Rank:	Paratrooper
Location:	Around Kabul
Conflict:	Invasion of Afghanistan

Sergeant-Major Motorized Rifle Battalion Afghanistan 1980

Not all Soviet infantry were well dressed for the bitter winter climate of Afghanistan during the Soviet Union's occupation, and morale was extremely depressed. This sergeant-major, however, has good kit, and he is seen here on guard duty over traffic movements in west Afghanistan. His head is protected by the fur ushanka, this having earflaps and the Communist Red Star centred on the fur front flap. Over his khaki infantry uniform he wears the standard Soviet-issue winter greatcoat, grey-brown in colour and deeply fly-fronted, without exposed buttons, to protect against wind chill (essential in Afghanistan's mountainous terrain). On his belt he has a Makarov PM pistol (the standard Soviet infantry pistol), an ammunition pouch (right hip), a respirator case and a bayonet for his AKM rifle, with wire-cutting scabbard clearly visible.

Date:	1980
Unit:	Motorized Rifle Battalion
Rank:	Sergeant-Major
Location:	West Afghanistan
Conflict:	Soviet occupation of Afghanistan

Sergeant
Spetsnaz
Afghan Mountains
1986

Though the Spetsnaz forces in Afghanistan were feared by the Mujahedeen, the Afghans' intimacy with the terrain meant that they suffered some heavy losses during the occupation. As their main roles were ambush or surveillance, camouflage uniforms were as standard. This soldier wears a hooded, one-piece leaf-pattern camouflage uniform of a type often worn by Soviet special forces. What is not typical is the calf-length high boots, based on patterns worn by soldiers back in Imperial Russia. On his utility belt hangs a 9mm PRI pistol in a black leather holster, an AK-series bayonet in a red plastic scabbard, an ammunition pouch and, behind his left hip, a kidney pouch containing survival supplies and demolitions. His weapon is the AKS-74, a 5.45mm (0.21in) version of the AK-47.

Date:	1986
Unit:	Spetsnaz
Rank:	Sergeant
Location:	Afghan Mountains
Conflict:	Soviet occupation of Afghanistan

Guerrilla Fighter Viet Minh Dien Bien Phu 1954

The First Indochina War (1945–1954) saw the Communist Viet Minh overthrow colonial French power through an impressive and highly structured programme of military and social resistance. The main fighting force was the 125,000-strong Chuc Luc, these men being supported in the field by village and regional militias. Chuc Luc uniforms were never standardized, but two types predominated. One was olive-green fatigues provided by sympathetic Communist China; and the other was the black 'pyjama' uniform, as shown here. This was simply a shirt and trousers dyed black, worn usually with a Vietnamese cork helmet, but here with a French slouch hat. Weaponry was of many sources, especially World War II-surplus and Chinese types. This guerrilla carries a French MAT 49 submachine gun, a standard French-issue submachine gun for infantry and para units.

Date:	1954
Unit:	Viet Minh
Rank:	Guerrilla Fighter
Location:	Dien Bien Phu
Conflict:	First Indochina War

Private
North
Vietnamese Army
Hanoi 1954

This soldier is seen during the victory celebrations in Hanoi following the collapse of French forces in Indochina after their cataclysmic defeat during the 55-day siege at Dien Bien Phu. The experience the NVA had gained in revolutionary war would stand them in good stead for the forthcoming conflict with South Vietnam and the United States. The appearance of this soldier is essentially little different from that of NVA soldiers in that later conflict. The olive-drab uniform is probably of local origin, the ankles of the trousers featuring buttons to keep out the insect life of the jungle floor. He holds aloft a hat made from woven reeds covered with cloth, little physical protection in itself, but cooling in the Vietnamese climate. His web belt holds a water bottle and a machete, while his rifle is a captured French 7.5mm (0.295in) MAS 1936.

Date:	1954
Unit:	North Vietnamese Army
Rank:	Private
Location:	Hanoi
Conflict:	First Indochina War

Guerrilla Fighter
Viet Cong
South Vietnam
1967

Popular history often presents the Viet Cong as ruthless fighters surviving on only a handful of rice a day. Ruthless they might have been, but the VC was a highly sophisticated political and military organization with advanced systems of supply and tactics. This soldier is wearing the classic black 'pyjamas' we now associate with the VC, though civilian clothing of many different types is equally, if not more, prevalent. He wears the palmleaf peasant hat, while his footwear consists of rubber sandals, often cut from car tyres. Rice is carried in a fairly large quantity in the roll around the body in the traditional Vietnamese way. Webbing would usually be, as here, a simple belt, with ammunition in belt pouches or in the distinctive 'ChiCom' chest pouches. His weapon is a Soviet RPG-2, which could destroy most enemy APCs and all but the heaviest tanks.

Date:	1966
Unit:	Viet Cong
Rank:	Guerrilla Fighter
Location:	South Vietnam
Conflict:	Vietnam War

Guerrilla Fighter
Viet Cong
South Vietnam
1967

The Soviet AK-47 assault rifle became almost symbolic of the Viet Cong and Communist cause during the Vietnam War. Though by no means as sophisticated or accurate as the US 5.56mm (0.22in) M16A1 rifle used by their enemies, it was incredibly dependable, easy to use, and could put out ferocious close-quarter firepower. Its reliability was such that many US soldiers used them as an alternative to the M16 which suffered from carbon-fouling and jamming and had to be meticulously cleaned each day. This guerrilla holds an AK-47 and carries ammunition for it in the 'ChiCom' chest pouches (for 'Chinese Communist' after the nation which pioneered the style) used by many Viet Cong. It was ideal for jungle warfare, as it was comfortable, each pouch holding two AK magazines, and was easy to keep clear of foliage when moving through the jungle.

Date:	1967
Unit:	Viet Cong
Rank:	Guerrilla Fighter
Location:	South Vietnam
Conflict:	Vietnam War

First Lieutenant ARVN South Vietnam 1970

Despite huge investment by the US in the materiel and training of the Army of the Republic of South Vietnam (ARVN), and despite having some truly élite units, ARVN never fulfilled its potential as a military force and was constantly weakened by factionalism and poor morale. This soldier is pictured in 1970, a time when the US was withdrawing from the Vietnam War and leaving South Vietnam to a fated future. His camouflage uniform is in the 'Tigerstripe' pattern, designed by the Vietnamese Marine Corps in 1959 and worn by many US Special Forces soldiers. It features a shirt and trousers, with a matching slouch hat displaying two gold blossoms, the rank marking of a first lieutenant. His webbing is Vietnamese-made and has nylon mesh panels instead of straps for coolness. His M16 ammunition is contained in the chest pouches, while on his US M1967 belt are two M26A2 fragmentation-grenades.

Date:	1970
Unit:	ARVN
Rank:	First Lieutenant
Location:	South Vietnam
Conflict:	Vietnam War

Senior Sergeant Artillery Arm Yugoslav Army Yugoslavia 1941

This senior sergeant wears the standard uniform of the Yugoslav infantry, though there should be some caution about using the word 'standard'. Yugoslavian military dress had its origins in Serbian uniform, which in turn was indebted to Austro-Hungarian and Imperial Russian uniforms, so that during the war, variations – particularly amongst officer dress – were common. This uniform is generally representative, though the colour could also be light- or field- grey. Here we have a single-breasted khaki tunic with fly front and four slash pockets covered with decorative flaps. The stand collar features the black colour of the artillery, as do the shoulder-straps in the edging. The trousers are tucked into long puttees, and he wears an officer's leather belt. The cap features the Yugoslav cockade; there were also three different types of steel helmet.

Date:	March 1941
Unit:	Artillery Arm
Rank:	Senior Sergeant
Theatre:	Balkans
Location:	Yugoslavia

309

Private
Infantry Division
Yugoslav Army
Yugoslavia 1941

The Yugoslav Army was disastrously inefficient in its resistance to the Axis take-over in 1941, and Yugoslavia was destined for years of brutal German reprisal actions and civil war which left over one million Yugoslav citizens and soldiers dead. This particular soldier strikes an archaic aspect in the age of Blitzkrieg, being dressed in the Serbian uniform of World War I. This was a double-breasted jacket with stand collar – whose colour indicated arm-of-service – baggy pantaloons tucked into knee-high puttees, black shoes and a French Adrian model helmet (motorized troops also wore the French helmet). During the early years of the war, many of these outdated tunics were replaced by single-breasted versions, and shoulder-straps began to display arm-of-service colours. The rifle is the Yugoslav 7.9mm (0.311in) M1924.

Date:	April 1941
Unit:	Infantry Division
Rank:	Private
Theatre:	Balkans
Location:	Yugoslavia

Captain
Infantry Regiment
Yugoslav Army
Yugoslavia 1941

Though this captain is wearing the more modern service tunic issued in the early 1940s (officers, however, had uniforms of a much finer cloth and a slightly greener colour) the ornamentation clearly casts a glance back into Imperial Russia. Chief amongst these features are the shoulder boards which are Imperial Russian in style, while an aiguillette across the shoulder and chest add some additional ceremony. As with lower ranks, arm-of-service is indicated by the stand-collar colour and the edging of the shoulder boards. For officers only, the colour of the stripe down the pantaloon legs and of the band around the cuff also gave arm-of-service. This officer's side cap features national cockade with a gilt metal cypher of King Peter I superimposed over the top. The same badge was also worn by officers on a kepi peaked cap.

Date:	April 1941
Unit:	Infantry Regiment
Rank:	Captain
Theatre:	Balkans
Location:	Yugoslavia

Captain Fighter Flight Yugoslav Air Force Yugoslavia 1941

The Yugoslav Air Force consisted of 419 aircraft at the outbreak of war, though many were obsolescent and had no significant impact against Axis occupation. This captain wears the grey-blue officers' service dress. This was a single-breasted tunic worn over a white shirt and black tie, with a matching pair of trousers and side cap. The rank of captain is shown on the shoulder boards (blue base, gold panel, dark-blue stripe down the centre and three gold pips) and in the three gold stripes on each cuff, above which is seen a small eagle to indicate that this wearer is a pilot (the badge on the right breast also shows that he is a qualified pilot). The medal on the left breast is the Yugoslav Order of the White Eagle. Officers were also issued with a double-breasted greatcoat, and in summer a white tunic and white cap-cover were an alternative form of dress.

Date:	April 1941
Unit:	Fighter Flight
Rank:	Captain
Theatre:	Balkans
Location:	Yugoslavia

Index

Note: Page numbers in **bold** refer to main entries.